THE *WEIRD* APOSTLE

RYAN C. LAMBERT

Copyright © 2024
Cover design and illustrations by: Kara Lambert

ISBN: 979-8-218-36900-2
Library of Congress Control Number: 2024903612

Publisher's Cataloging-in-Publication (Provided by Cassidy Cataloguing Services, Inc.)
Names: Lambert, Ryan C., author.
Title: The weird apostle : [the strange Jewish mission of a global game changer] / Ryan C. Lambert.
Description: [Roswell, Georgia] : [Ryan Lambert Forum], [2024] | Subtitle from back cover. | Includes bibliographical references.
Identifiers: ISBN: 979-8-218-36900-2 (paperback) | LCCN: 2024903612
Subjects: LCSH: Paul, the Apostle, Saint--Jewish interpretations. | Paul, the Apostle, Saint--Biblical teaching. | Paul, the Apostle, Saint--Correspondence. | Judaism--Relations--Christianity. | Jesus Christ--Jewishness. | Apostles. | BISAC: RELIGION / Biblical Commentary / New Testament / Paul's Letters. | RELIGION / Biblical Studies / New Testament / Paul's Letters. | RELIGION / Christian Theology / History.
Classification: LCC: BS2506.3 .L36 2024 | DDC: 225.92--dc23

For Stardust

"Hope's not dead, love's not haunted, and . . .
I bet my life on it too."
—Highbeams

"May the God of hope fill you with all joy and peace."
—Paul

CONTENTS

INTRODUCTION

Drinks with a Global Game Changer

It's a few minutes after 5:00 p.m. on a Thursday. I arrive at From the Earth Brewing Company early to grab one of the picnic tables out front and enjoy the fresh air, the light spring breeze, and the beautiful sunset outside. I'm a little nervous about our meeting, so I order my normal, a Goin' Out West IPA. It's nice to settle in and have a few sips before he arrives.

He's a couple minutes late. When he arrives, he's a bit scattered and jittery. Not nervous, but distracted. I ask if he had trouble finding the place. He immediately squares in on my eyes. "Ryan, it's nice to meet you. What's on your mind?" No small talk. The Weird Apostle is all business.

He declines my offer to buy him a drink. I take another sip and straighten up.

"Paul, you are likely among the twenty most influential humans in history," I say. "And you are certainly in an elite class of Jews, probably right behind Jesus and arguably parallel with Abraham and Moses regarding your impact upon the world."

Paul stops me. "I appreciate the compliments, but, please, what do you want to discuss with me?"

I adjust my seat again, take another sip, and realize Paul has zero interest in my attempt to frame the conversation. So, I dial it in.

"I'd really like to understand you and your letters better. It's been almost two thousand years since you wrote them, and I'm sure those who have attempted to understand you have missed some things. Where have we gone astray?"

Paul takes a deep breath and looks slightly to the left. His eye catches the TV screens inside the restaurant. The Atlanta Braves' baseball pregame show is on. He stares at it for a long five seconds. I turn my eyes to where his are, crack a smile, and casually joke, "Do you like baseball? That could help rehabilitate your reputation in the Jewish community."

Paul is unfazed by my humor—and seemingly disinterested in the fact that American Jews love baseball. But a slight drop in his shoulders signals that my comment about his reputation in the Jewish community may have stung.

His eyes slowly turn back to mine. "I had no idea my letters would circulate so widely. And it boggles my mind that what I wrote then would continue to be discussed long after my life. It's all very strange to me." He looks to the right, his eyes tracking the growing crowd of people gathering to play cornhole and relax on this cool but comfortable spring evening.

Paul's eyes continue bouncing around the crowd, but mine are fixed on his. "What do you mean when you say it's all so strange?" I ask.

Abruptly, he stands up, pushes away from the table, and turns toward the counter. In a surprisingly relaxed tone, he says, "Actually, I think I will have a drink."

The servers would've happily taken his order from our seats, but he heads to the bar, leaving me alone again at the table. But this is good. While I wait for him to return, it softly hits me that Paul is not a mythical figure. He's a human—just like me. After all, at least he's having a drink with me now. I feel my tension lower.

When he returns, Paul notices my hat—a plain Georgia peach hat. "That's a sharp cap," he says awkwardly, reducing my anxiety even more. *What a strange guy*, I think.

Paul settles back on the bench and sips what looks like the Midnight Rider porter. How poetic.

He resumes. "From what I can tell, a big problem with how people understand my letters is that folks try to make me look too much like them. They read what I wrote through the lens of their problems, their issues, and their times. I wrote letters that addressed issues in my day. And while certain topics can resurface, much of what I wrote had to do with specific things we were dealing with at that time, not this time or any time in between."

Now we're cooking. This is what I was looking for.

"Much of what is written and said about me makes little sense," Paul adds. "Things are frequently attributed to me that are the opposite of what I meant to communicate. It's weird. Very weird."

And with that word—"weird"—something clicks. I look down and focus on my IPA as I absorb his words. And I realize something.

Paul has been made to look too much like us.

So much about the global game changer sitting across from me has been oversimplified and pressed into categories that were foreign to him. Mainstream, historical views of Paul are, strangely, not strange enough. A key to understanding this world-class influencer would be to turn the table. As odd as it feels, I realize Paul needs to be made "weird" once again.

Thankfully, From the Earth is a real place—with fantastic beer. And the picnic tables out front really are an ace when the weather is good. Everything else about that story is fiction. But would such a conversation with Paul, were it to happen in real life, be so far-fetched?

I have no problem with any answer you have in your mind. And I imagine every reader is thinking something a little different.

But I think we can get on the same page about two things regarding Paul:

1. Paul was weird.
2. Paul was a global game changer.

And one more thing we can likely agree on:

3. It's impossible to calculate what the world would look like without the presence of Paul and his letters.

Many people do not embrace the thirteen letters attributed to Paul[1] in the New Testament as holy Scripture. But everyone who has lived on planet Earth in the past two thousand years has been impacted by this unique, strange Jewish man.

Material written by or about Paul comprises half the content in the New Testament, one of the most influential sources that shaped our society today. As Daniel Langton aptly stated in his book *The Apostle Paul in the Jewish Imagination*, Paul's letters are "probably the most minutely examined collection of correspondence in the history of Western civilization."[2] Take Paul from history, and things would look a lot different.

My imagined one-on-one with Paul at my favorite neighborhood brewpub in Roswell, Georgia, could be far from reality if such a meeting occurred. Perhaps in an actual, modern meeting with Paul, he would acknowledge that his interpreters have largely captured the essence of his message.

My tale expresses what I believe is more probable. I think Paul would convey tremendous confusion and disappointment about how he has been understood. Oddly, in Paul's view, the standard picture of him would be weird because, essentially, Paul's interpreters have not allowed Paul to be Paul.

To gain a clearer understanding of the apostle and the modern implications of his letters, we need to allow Paul to be the weird character he was. I don't mean we need to make him more complicated to understand than he already is. God forbid.

Even Paul's like-minded contemporaries had a difficult time understanding him. Speaking of Paul's letters, another New Testament author said, "There are some things in them that are hard to understand."[3] The last thing we want to do is add additional filters and further obscure Paul. Strangely, my take is that making Paul weird will remove filters and magnify our vision of him.

The idea of making Paul weird did not originate with me. For the past few years, I've observed several Paul scholars, such as Matthew Novenson[4] and Matthew Thiessen, using the phrase "making Paul weird." Novenson and Thiessen are examples of scholars working on an academic level to substantiate this idea with cutting-edge research by reframing Paul within Judaism.[5] In Thiessen's excellent book *A Jewish Paul*,[6] he titles the first chapter "Making Paul Weird Again."

So maybe something is stirring here, like a "make Paul weird again" movement. Sounds like a good slogan! But, seriously, challenging the prevailing view of Paul and making him weird again is no easy task. And pushback should be expected. After all, what we're talking about serves as a challenge to assumptions about Paul that run deep. Excavating such premises can be not only laborious, but also treacherous.

It can be terrifying to question what we are sure of. And for a long time, both Christians and Jews have been convinced certain things about Paul are indisputable. There has been no need to debate ideas about Paul, such as:

- Paul used to be a Pharisee. But when he converted to Christianity, he finally found the grace and mercy his soul never found in Judaism.
- Saul the Jew became Paul the Christian and started a new religion called Christianity.

- To Paul, all that mattered was Jesus. All other aspects of his identity, and the identities of his followers, no longer mattered.

Yup, those ideas are familiar—and for many Jews and Christians, they are a sure thing. But what if those familiar ideas about Paul obscure, rather than reveal, who Paul was and the ideas he aimed to advance?

So here's what I mean when I say we need to make Paul weird again. Paul, also known as Saint Paul, is one of the most influential humans in history. Yet he is also one of the most misunderstood and misrepresented characters of all time. Historically, Paul has been made to appear like a Western-minded, modern Christian. In this book, I challenge those largely uncontested ideas, suggesting Paul was a Torah-observant Jewish man who functioned entirely within Judaism as the apostle to the Gentiles.

Our society has much to gain by doing the hard work of reframing Paul in terms that are less familiar to us but more faithful to his ancient Jewish and Greco-Roman context. Understanding him in these terms can also help counter historical trends and modern voices that use Paul's writings, intentionally or otherwise, to advance anti-Semitic and anti-Judaism perspectives.

As we go on this journey together, I will present seven ways to make Paul weird again:

1. He had a weird upbringing.
2. He had a weird flash moment.
3. He had a weird mission.
4. He had a weird message.
5. He had a weird view of time.
6. He had a weird lifestyle.
7. He had a weird rule.

No doubt, there is plenty more weird stuff to discuss about Paul—and I intend to cover that in a follow-up volume to this book[7]— but starting here will help narrow the gap between the familiar, mainstream view of Paul and the historical, real-deal man.

Oh, and one more thing before we start. We're going to get into some pretty deep conversations about Paul. That can be fun. But it can sometimes make our brains hurt. This book is not meant to be an intellectual burden or exercise. Yes, I hope it will challenge your thinking on Paul. And I also hope *The Weird Apostle* will positively affect real, on-the-ground relationships.

Various components of Paul's letters have practical value and tangible relevance in modern times. That's why I wrote this book. Paul's letters can be understood in a way that brings diverse groups together while respecting differences. For too long, Paul's letters have been used as tools of division—primarily between Christians and Jews. I hope making Paul weird again can serve as a beam in a growing bridge-building movement that is dedicated to improving those relations.

So, let's do this. Here's to making Paul weird again!

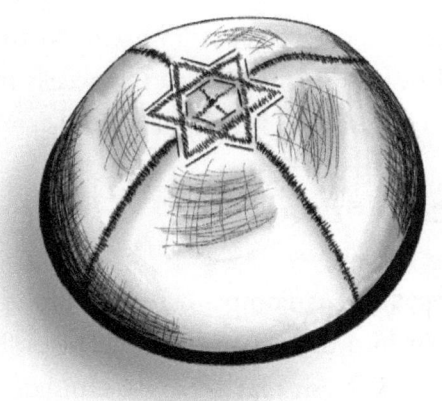

CHAPTER 1

Paul's Weird Upbringing

Paul's identity as a Pharisee was far from wasted time

CROSBY, STILLS, NASH . . . AND PAUL

Crosby, Stills & Nash[8] (CSN) was an iconic folk-rock band popular in the 1970s and '80s. CSN continued producing music well into the 2000s, but their best material, in my opinion, was their early stuff.

Because I was born in 1975, I wasn't in tune with '70s and early '80s music until I was older, but I have come to love music from that era. The emphasis on harmony and great songwriting was on a special plane back then. I could go on about the Bee Gees; Earth, Wind & Fire; and the Eagles. As you will see throughout this book, I can get carried away when it comes to great music. But let's get back to Crosby, Stills, Nash . . . and Paul.

One of my favorite CSN songs from that period, beautifully written and masterfully performed, is "Wasted on the Way." It had been a while since I heard this song, but a few weeks into writing this book, I heard it again. Strangely, I thought of Paul.

ABUNDANT CHUTZPAH

My stepdad, Pop, lives in Pompano Beach, Florida. On a recent visit, we rode his boat into the Atlantic Ocean, just off the coast. Pop played a Crosby, Stills & Nash playlist as we cruised. When "Wasted on the Way" came on, I smiled and leaned in. As I listened, unexpectedly, I thought of Paul's strange self-identification as a Pharisee.

I felt a bit like a fanatic at that moment. *Just enjoy the boat ride and stop thinking about Paul*, I thought. But my mind was on the book, so I went with it.

Certainly, "Wasted on the Way" has nothing to do with Paul. It doesn't even mention God or the Bible. But the lyrics made me think of what Paul's experience may have been like as a youth and, strangely, how many have classified his upbringing.

If you don't know or haven't heard "Wasted on the Way" in a while, look it up and give it a listen. It's a beautiful piece that reflects on how a person spent earlier seasons of life and how they want to better invest their time moving forward. Those earlier seasons, in some sense, were wasted. Now, it's time to get things right by living life with a greater sense of bravery and love.

Why did I think of Paul when I heard "Wasted on the Way"? Indeed, the connection largely emanated from my overcharged romantic imagination. But more concretely, I identified two connections. One has to do with what I imagine about Paul's personality, especially in his youth. The second concerns what many assume about "wasted time" in Paul's life.

Paul's letters and the book of Acts signal that his personality included an overflow of chutzpah. We see indications of Paul's nerve in the following ways:

- He described himself as highly zealous in multiple stages of his life.[9]
- He got into all kinds of trouble, based on his own report.[10]
- He had frequent friction with others.[11]

Yes, these examples point to Paul as someone who had the kind of courage "Wasted on the Way" envies. His gall was likely evident well before he became an adult. Thus, as a youth, it's probable Paul was full of what every game-changing influencer abounds with: a sense of inquiry and curiosity.

I think it's fair to imagine Paul as the type who was full of questions and perhaps struggled with self-regulation. I bet he was a handful as a kid. And an author with a surprising background also envisioned such restlessness in young Paul.

SHOLEM ASCH ON PAUL

Sholem Asch (1880–1957) was a prolific Yiddish writer who produced many works on Jewish spirituality. Asch was one of many post-Enlightenment Jewish authors who dared to engage with Christian topics. However, he was unique among Jewish thinkers in his day (and heavily criticized) for framing Christian ideas and characters in a positive light.

In 1943, Asch produced a controversial novel about Paul called *The Apostle*. Using information from the New Testament as a basis for an imaginative story about the life of the apostle, Asch also pictured the young Paul as full of zeal, questions, and nerve:

Very early in his manhood he began to mold his life consciously in the spirit of his exalted vision of his destiny. He took certain vows and practiced sacred fasts. Like a Nazirite, he sundered himself from the surrounding world, spending his nights as well as his days in the study of sacred and secular books. . . . Very often he would work himself into a condition of ecstasy which resembled a trance; he would fall down, and foam would break out on his lips. His parents were terrified by the recurrence of these incidents, but they could not persuade him to alter his manner of life. This was his decision, and no one could swerve him from it. . . . He began to speak of Jerusalem and his need to go there, so that he might sit at the feet of Rabban Gamaliel and drink from the purest source of Jewish lore.[12]

Asch's description of Paul's youth was fictitious, but his creative estimation of a young Paul is reasonable based on information about the apostle contained in the New Testament.

It's important to underscore that Asch did not embrace Paul's messianic claims. But he did value Paul's story and framed the apostle as a Jewish character. And for Asch, Paul's charisma as a youth served as a preview of what was to come.

WASTING TIME AS A PHARISEE?

"Wasted on the Way" sparked my curiosity not only into Paul's temperament as a youth, but also at how his upbringing as a Pharisee is typically visualized. Before we get into that, let's get grounded in this idea that Paul was a Pharisee. On this point, there is not much debate.

Two New Testament texts identify Paul as a Pharisee:

- In Acts 23:6, Luke[13] recorded that Paul said, "I *am* a Pharisee."

- In Philippians 3:5, Paul listed "Pharisee" as a personal credential that he expected his audience to find presently meaningful.

Here's a fun fact you can keep in your pocket the next time you play cards with friends who like talking about the Bible: Paul is one of only two people in history who claimed to be a Pharisee and whose personal writings we still have. The other person is the Jewish historian Josephus. And though Josephus wrote that he was a Pharisee, some historians question this claim.[14] All other references to Pharisees come from later rabbinic sources, the Dead Sea Scrolls, and stories found in the Gospels and Acts. It's pretty cool that Paul's letter to the Philippians is the only firsthand source we have from an individual historians agree was a Pharisee.

Hopefully, we're having fun so far.

But here's where things get tricky: These two New Testament sources associated Paul with being a Pharisee well into his vocation as an apostle for the Jesus movement.

Yes, things are getting weird. The Apostle Paul continued thinking of himself as a Pharisee? Did that make him a Christian Pharisee? How was this possible? Those are contradictory terms, right?

There are some things we know to be true of the Pharisees. The Pharisees were the epitome of hypocrisy and self-righteousness. They represented a religious environment devoid of spiritual life. They may even be associated with religious violence and murder. This is how most people think about the Pharisees.

Thus, because Paul was raised as a Pharisee, it's not unusual for his upbringing to be sized up as not only weird but *wasted*.

We've raised what may feel like an irritating question with all we assume to be inherently true about the Pharisees. But, again, why would Paul the Apostle continue identifying with this group *after* he became a follower of Jesus?

THE JOY OF BEING WRONG

In Adam Grant's book *Think Again,*[15] he titles chapter 3 "The Joy of Being Wrong: The Thrill of Not Believing Everything You Think." Grant's point is that imperfect, limited, or sometimes incorrect knowledge often stunts our ability to grow and learn. As Grant emphasizes, sometimes we should heed the words of the Star Wars character Yoda, "You must unlearn what you have learned."

Well, we *know* some things about the Pharisees that we might need to rethink. Common assumptions about the Pharisees have not only obscured how we understand Paul, but also dramatically affected relationships between Christians and Jews. The stakes regarding how we understand ancient Pharisees and their modern descendants are high.

And before we dig into the details of the Pharisees and Paul's weird background, here's one more cage rattler: I don't think we would even know of a character named the Apostle Paul if not for his upbringing as a Pharisee. It was that important in positively shaping who Paul became. Thus, a misguided view of the Pharisees directly affects how we understand Paul. As Jewish scholar Pamela Eisenbaum has aptly said, "For the person who wishes to understand Paul in historically accurate terms, it is essential to have a historically accurate understanding of Pharisees."[16]

THE DISTORTED "BAD GUYS"

What comes to mind when you hear the word "Pharisee"?

For most, this word represents negative concepts like "empty religion," "enemy of Jesus," and "hypocrite." It's no secret or revelation that Christians have primarily perpetuated this representation. In an article titled "Your Inner Pharisee," posted by the popular Christian organization the Gospel Coalition, Josh Moody says this about Pharisees: "They are *other* people—bad people, legalists, judgmentalists, those who attack Christ and defend fake, hypocritical religion. 'Hypocrites' is the most important descriptor. . . . In the end, the Pharisees were even willing to support murder to accomplish their desires."[17]

In Christian space, one of the highest forms of criticism one can dish out or receive is through association with the term "Pharisee." But Christians are not alone in equating "Pharisee" with "hypocrisy." Such usage has long been part of the mainstream vernacular. Take a moment and jump on dictionary.com. Among the synonyms for "hypocrite," guess what word is on the list? Yup, "Pharisee" is right there. The association between Pharisees and hypocritical behavior is embedded deep within mainstream consciousness, even on the level of our dictionaries.

It may come as a surprise that not all people understand Pharisees unfavorably. For modern religious Jews, the Pharisees represent a group with a deep love for God who had the spiritual flexibility and wisdom to survive the calamities of the first century of the Common Era, when the Jerusalem Temple was destroyed and the Jewish people were exiled from the land of Israel. From this vantage point, the Pharisees are viewed as heroic forebearers who kept Judaism alive when it faced the possibility of extinction. But those who view the Pharisees positively represent a small minority.

For generations, the Pharisees have been broadly cast as the bad guys of the New Testament who opposed Jesus and his followers at every turn. And for just as long, it has been assumed that being a Pharisee was something Paul was overjoyed to extract from his identity once he became a follower of Jesus. Endless examples of this traditional portrayal of Paul show up in Christian commentaries, books, sermons, and even in casual conversations.

A sharp example of the cancerous nature of all things pharisaical is in the 2012 book *Pharisectomy: How to Joyfully Remove Your Inner Pharisee and Other Religiously Transmitted Diseases*[18] by pastor and author Peter Haas. Highly influential and well-known Christian pastors praised this book. I read it cover to cover, but the title says it all: Many people feel the Pharisees are a religious disease that needs to be removed.

Haas, however, is just one of many modern influencers who continues perpetuating the stereotype that the Pharisees represent the worst form of spiritual malady. Just do a quick Google search for "modern Pharisees" and you will find plenty of articles from highly regarded Christian sources that frame the Pharisees as the ultimate example of what *not* to be as a person of faith.

One more example of this is poignant. In his 2022 book *Not in It to Win It*, Pastor Andy Stanley goes even further than Haas in his unfavorable portrayal of how Paul was raised and trained as a Pharisee:

> Paul, who prided himself on being the most law-abiding Pharisee in the Middle East, believed he was acting on God's behalf when he assumed the role of inquisitor and executioner. . . . Before his conversion, Paul was a living example of what the old covenant looked like and behaved like. When operating under the authority of the old covenant, he was free to track down, arrest, torture, and execute apostate Jews. According to his understanding of the Hebrew Scriptures, his unbridled cruelty was God's will.[19]

Pastor Stanley's words are bold, and the implications are clear. Being a Pharisee and living life under the old covenant encouraged and justified Paul's behavior as an inquisitor and executioner, and it warranted torture, executions, and cruel treatment.

For those unfamiliar with Pastor Stanley, he is no outlier. He has been one of the world's leading Christian voices for nearly thirty years. His perspective on the Pharisees and Paul's upbringing is influential and representative of how many Christians see things: The Pharisees were religious (and some would say violent) hypocrites, forming a stark contrast to the grace-saturated message of Jesus.

Let me clarify that I am not accusing Haas or Stanley of anti-Semitism. I don't know either of them personally. And I doubt either of them hates Jews or wants to see Jews harmed. I imagine both men would be quick to clarify that they are not pinning their description of ancient Pharisees on modern Jews.

But here's the problem. History has not been so nuanced in its thinking.

It is a mainstream assumption to draw a straight line from ancient Pharisees to present-day Jews—regardless of the era. In other words, whether it is historically accurate or not, it is common to visualize a timeless link between the Pharisees and today's Jewish people. Thus, continuing to hold up the Pharisees as the ultimate religious villains also casts a negative, dangerous light upon modern Jews.

With this rhetoric still circulating strongly today, it is no surprise that it remains a largely uncontested conclusion that Paul's upbringing as a Pharisee was "wasted time" living in a spiritually bankrupt religious realm at best and a breeding ground for terrorist-like activity at worst.

However, recent studies on the ancient Pharisees have led a growing number of scholars, historians, and regular folks like you and me to question the prevailing viewpoint of the Pharisees. New analyses of the New Testament and ancient sources have led many to question long-held assumptions about this ancient group. This new research has included reflections on how negative stereotypes of the Pharisees have affected much more than our understanding of Paul's upbringing. Unfavorable tropes about the Pharisees have also fueled anti-Jewish sentiment, which all too often in history led to concrete acts of violence toward Jewish people.

TIME WELL SPENT: HOW PAUL WAS RAISED AS A PHARISEE

Paul's upbringing and background in Judaism, as a Pharisee, is undoubtedly weird from the vantage point of most people. That's understandable, because most people don't possess a firsthand awareness of what it's like to be raised in an ancient, or even modern, religious Jewish community.

However, due to the prominence of the Jewish people in the Bible, non-Jews have a significant interest in Jews and Judaism. Throughout history, though, many people have drawn conclusions about Jews and Judaism without directly interacting with real Jews and primary Jewish sources. Sadly, this has led to many misunderstandings about the Jewish way of life—in both ancient and modern times.

Judaism has evolved significantly over the past two thousand years. Today, many Orthodox Jews still live with similar values as the Pharisees regarding their devotion to the Torah (the laws found in the first five books of the Bible) and Jewish traditions. But being raised as an ancient Pharisee or as an Orthodox Jew in modern times does not inherently include being a carrier of an RTD (religiously transmitted disease). Too many people still sympathize with this viewpoint.

Growing up as a Pharisee was not wasted time for Paul. And it's not wasted time for today's Orthodox Jews. Like every past or present group, the Pharisees had their bad apples. But Paul's upbringing as a Pharisee, while foreign and strange to most of us, did not teach him a way of life he was relieved to be rescued from. No, Paul was not bred to be an executioner. As a Pharisee, he was taught to love God with every breath. And his upbringing gave him an outlook and skills that positioned him to be a global advocate for the principles of Judaism.

While we still have more questions than answers about the Pharisees, a growing body of evidence from ancient sources indicates these attributes about them:

- They were serious students of the Bible.
- They affirmed that the Bible included the Jewish prophets and Wisdom books (Psalms, Proverbs, etc.). This was not true of all Jewish groups at the time.
- They aimed to be precise in their interpretation of the Torah.

- They were committed to oral traditions handed down to them from earlier generations.
- They were popular and influential among ordinary people.
- They were considered progressive because of their efforts to make exclusive purity practices accessible to regular Jews.
- They had political influence.
- They were represented across social and economic classes.
- They were known for living righteous lives.
- They believed in the resurrection of the dead.
- They believed in the afterlife.

The features of the Pharisees that are absent from ancient sources are as important as the ones that are present. Josephus, the Dead Sea Scrolls, the New Testament, and later rabbinic writings give us no reason to believe the Pharisees encouraged violence, cruelty, or torture. Such behavior among the Pharisees, and among modern Jews, would be condemned and considered widely deviant.

The point of this chapter is not to exhaustively study the characteristics of the ancient Pharisees or modern Jews. There are some great resources available if you'd like to do that.[20] The point of this chapter is to better comprehend Paul by gaining a more historically probable understanding of the Pharisees. To do so, there are two more fundamental ideas about Pharisees we need to rethink to gain a clearer view of the Weird Apostle.

THE FLEXIBLE, LIBERAL PHARISEES —SAY WHAT?

The Pharisees had a well-known reputation for valuing an exact and precise interpretation of the Torah. However, it may be a surprise to learn the Pharisees were also criticized for being too flexible and lenient in their interpretations. Some historians think the Pharisees are the group that the Dead Sea Scroll community referred to critically as "seekers after smooth things" (or, alternatively, "givers of smooth interpretations").[21] Further denunciation of the Pharisees' interpretive style is evident in the Gospels when Jesus criticized the Pharisees for bending Scripture in such a fashion that led to an inversion of priorities (see Mark 7:1–23). On the leniency of the Pharisees, Pamela Eisenbaum's words are helpful:

> I suspect that it may come as a surprise when I say that the gospel writers view the Pharisees as too lenient—a surprise precisely because the Christian stereotype of the Pharisees is that they are legalistic and literalistic, following every precept of the Torah to an exacting degree. . . . That is why Jesus says, "Unless your righteousness exceeds that of the Scribes and Pharisees, you will never enter the kingdom of heaven."[22]

For a long time, I wondered about the statement Eisenbaum refers to when Jesus said his disciples' righteousness must *exceed* that of the Pharisees (see Matt 5:20). How could any group be more righteous than the Pharisees? While Jesus upheld the authority of the Pharisees (see Matt 23:1–2), it appears he had some concerns about the degree of flexibility exercised in some of their decisions. This point helped me see the Pharisees differently. Oddly, in the minds of their contemporaries, the Pharisees applied Scripture *too liberally*.

This is an important way we need to rethink the Pharisees. They were firmly committed to faithfully interpreting the Torah. But they also were well known to be adaptable and creative in their *halacha*—a Hebrew term referring to how the Torah is "walked out."

All of this is important as we consider Paul. As a Pharisee, he was raised to treasure the Torah. But he also learned to be creative, flexible, and, some in his day might say, a bit liberal regarding how the Torah was to be lived. Again, Eisenbaum provides a helpful perspective:

Perhaps Paul had a more flexible view of the Torah to start with, and thus perhaps his seemingly "looser" interpretations of various commandments derive from his training as a Pharisee. In other words, it is not necessary to see his Damascus road experience as the point of origin for the apostle's more creative interpretations of Scripture. His more adaptive teachings on Torah as apostle to the Gentiles were most likely learned while he was a Pharisee.[23]

This is huge. Paul's letters are filled with instructions for his non-Jewish audience regarding how they should live according to various Torah principles *as non-Jews*. Here's a strange reality to consider: Many modern Christians observe a lot of the Torah without even knowing it because Paul, like a good Pharisee, provided accessible Torah instruction for non-Jews within his letters.

Paul's ministry to non-Jews was an unprecedented enterprise that required a creative and adaptive approach to the Torah. Paul learned this as a Pharisee. His upbringing was not wasted time.

THE (MAYBE NOT SO) LEGALISTIC PHARISEES

The second big thing a lot of people know about the Pharisees is that they were the epitome of legalism. We need to rethink this point also.

It is widely assumed that, as a Pharisee, Paul was raised to believe one gained favor and good standing with God through the accumulation of good works. This is commonly referred to as "legalism." Some may be more familiar with legalism's sister descriptors, "salvation by works" or "works-based righteousness."

Many Christians have a triangular view of the relationship between the Pharisees, legalism, and Paul: The Pharisees were legalists. Paul used to be a Pharisee. On the Damascus Road, Paul stopped being a legal-istic Pharisee and became a grace-oriented Christian. Moving forward, Paul no longer believed one earns their standing with God through the accumulation of good deeds. Thus, Paul's Christian gospel was a foil to Pharisaic legalism.

But there's a foundational flaw in this geometry, which gives birth to significant misunderstandings. The Pharisees were not legalists.

Several modern Christian thinkers are dedicated to challenging this deeply rooted assumption, such as Kent Yinger in his book *The Phari-sees* (emphasis my own):

> Our review of the Pharisees in Jewish literature did not support this legalistic portrait. . . . True, they were known for their exceeding akribeia, their commitment to the precise interpre-tation of the law's commands and prohibitions, but this was not typically viewed as their gateway to grace. . . . Instead, the intense focus on detailed performance of God's will in Torah was built on a foundation of **God's electing grace to Israel** and was seen as the way to walk in faithfulness to this God, not the way to earn his love.[24]

Yinger's research posits that the portrayal of the Pharisees as legalists cannot be supported. Instead, he emphasizes that the relevant ancient sources point to the Pharisees' well-known dedication to careful Torah observance was built on a foundation of God's electing grace to Israel. That is a very different picture of the environment from which Paul was supposedly delivered. As weird as it may sound, as a Pharisee, Paul learned God was gracious, merciful, and compassionate.

The fact is that there is little, and some would say zero, evidence to indicate the Pharisees were legalists. They did not believe one earned salvation, righteousness, or standing with God through good works. Thus, if that's not what the Pharisees believed, then it's highly improb-able that's what Paul was raised to believe too. And if this was not Paul's belief, then we need to reconsider the idea that Paul's gospel message served to counter legalism.

We'll look closer at Paul's weird message in chapter 4. But for now, let's focus on this: Ancient sources that we have access to do not label the Pharisees as legalists. However, they do suggest, as a growing number of scholars emphasize, that the Pharisees believed deeply in the grace and mercy of God.

PUMP THOSE BRAKES, PLEASE

It might sound like I'm going too far in flattening the opposition between Jesus, Paul, and the Pharisees that is plentiful in the New Testament. So let's answer a few questions you might have.

Did Jesus, Paul, and other Pharisees have sharp differences? They sure did. And we observe some of those differences recorded in the New Testament. Matthew 23:13 contains some well-known bitter criticism from Jesus toward the scribes and Pharisees: "But woe to you, scribes and Pharisees, hypocrites! For you shut the kingdom of heaven in people's faces. For you neither enter yourselves nor allow those who would enter to go in."

That's a harsh statement. And it should be tough for anyone to swallow. However, the reality is that it is normal among Jewish groups, both in ancient and modern times, to express differences with such intense, exaggerated language. Inter-Jewish criticism within Jewish texts is not always expressed so nicely. Other non-Jesus-oriented groups had differences with the Pharisees as well. Like the Gospels, they did not use flowery language in their criticism. As Richard Horsley noted in his important book *The Pharisees and the Temple-State of Judea*, "The Qumran Scrolls (a.k.a. 'Dead Sea Scrolls' possessed by the 'Essenes') are no less hostile to the 'interpreters of smooth things' (likely referring to the Pharisees) than the Gospels are to 'the scribes and Pharisees.'"[25]

Were there corrupt and hypocritical Pharisees? Yes, there were. But every group, religious or otherwise, has people who are poor representatives of the principles their tribe represents. Again, Yinger's perspective is helpful. He says:

> Were the Pharisees hypocrites? Our answer is yes and no. Yes, some Pharisees may well have been hypocrites, as is usually the case with any religious group. Yes, from Jesus' perspective and that of the early church, the Pharisees were hypocrites by claiming to love and listen to God, yet they refused to listen to the one whom God had sent. No, as a group, Pharisees were not characterized by hypocrisy. And most importantly, Jesus' accusations need to be understood as invective, as a form of generalized and exaggerated speech to warn against someone or something.[26]

So, yes, the Pharisees, Jesus, and Paul had their differences. And, yes, there were hypocritical Pharisees. But the differences had nothing to do with legalism, and the hypocrisy Jesus confronted did not characterize the Pharisees as a whole.

The arguments between Jesus and the Pharisees centered on *how* to walk out God's commandments. They did not argue about the importance of God's mercy, grace, and forgiveness; this was fundamental to the fabric of Judaism and the Torah. And their agreement on central principles made possible some fierce exchanges. The Gospels are filled with such heated encounters, but these tense moments also point to the commonalities in their orientation.

Typically, you argue and debate with folks whose outlook and way of life are comparable to yours. Mormons don't dialog with Muslims about the nature of the afterlife, and Muslims don't ask Catholics for their take on divorce. But different Baptist groups do press each other on such topics. That's because they are in the same general camp.

The Pharisees were curious about Jesus's viewpoints on various topics because they had much in common, although that degree of overlap is debated. Many scholars surmise Jesus was most closely aligned with the Pharisees out of all the ancient sects of Judaism. Thus, it's no surprise Jesus appointed Paul the Pharisee to be his chief ambassador to the non-Jewish world.

Not all Jewish groups in antiquity emphasized the importance of prophets like Isaiah, Jeremiah, and Ezekiel. But the Pharisees did. Because the Pharisees affirmed the entire Old Testament, including the prophetic writings, their sensibilities included the hope and expectation of a messianic redeemer and an idyllic, future age that included non-Jews embracing Israel's God.

And that pharisaic value is displayed frequently in Paul's letters, as he naturally and repeatedly references the Jewish prophets to substantiate his points.

This may grind some gears, but here's what I'm suggesting. Paul's pharisaical upbringing, weird as it may seem to us, was essential to the success of his mission, making him well suited to bring a Jewish message of redemption to the world. We can conclude with confidence that if not for Paul's upbringing, he would not have possessed the outlook and tools needed to be the global game changer he was.

HOW PAUL'S WEIRD BACKGROUND CHANGES THE GAME

Let's face it, the Pharisees have been demonized as a group. For many generations, historians, scholars, theologians, pastors, and average folks like you and me have instinctually associated the Pharisees with the worst kind of religious expression. But the Pharisees are not worthy of the deeply negative symbolism attached to their name.

Paul was raised as a Pharisee. For most of us, that seems weird and foreign. That's okay. What's not okay is to interpret Paul's upbringing as time wasted in a spiritually contaminated environment.

Instead, Paul's upbringing provided a foundation that prepared him to be the apostle to the Gentiles. He was taught to question, press, and find the most exact interpretation of the Torah possible. He was taught to love God and his commandments. He was taught to consider creative and practical solutions to complex problems regarding walking out one's commitment to God. And he was trained to anticipate an age when not just Jews but all people would have shalom with God and each other. All this he learned as a Pharisee.

If not for Paul's pharisaic upbringing, he would not have been situated to be the ambassador for the Jesus movement that he was. And imagine how different the world might look without Paul's impact. Some may think the world would have been better off. Based on the countless ways Paul's letters have been utilized to justify various forms of hatred, that's understandable. But I'm not sure we would want to live in a world unaffected by Paul.

Not only was Paul a high-profile emissary for the Jesus movement, but his efforts also had a trailblazing effect on the advancement and establishment of Judeo-Christian ethics and values in the Western world. While many have not been personally persuaded by Paul's message, everyone in the Western world has benefitted from the societal implementation of Pauline concepts such as justice, forgiveness, and enduring love.

It will be a positive, life-giving game changer if negative stereotyping and generalizing of the Pharisees come to an end. They were not the bad boys of the New Testament. And they should not be seen as synonymous with hypocrisy. We will understand the Gospels, Paul, and this important ancient group better if we discontinue defining them in terms that (wrongly) centralize their inherent crookedness.

GAME-CHANGING ACTION

I assume most people reading this book have lived enough to experience the pain and discomfort of being mischaracterized or misrepresented. This is one of the worst human experiences, especially if distorted information goes public.

Twisted presentations of groups or individuals do significant damage. However, most of the time, a warped reputation is not life-threatening. Being stereotyped negatively has a high cost, but it typically does not endanger your life or community. This has not been the case for the Jewish people. Their genealogical connection with the Pharisees, both physically and spiritually, has cost them dearly.

Demonizing stereotypes rooted in tropes about the Pharisees have made it all too easy for Jews to be the scapegoats for countless calamities and afflictions experienced by their occupiers, stronger neighbors, and host nations. Because the term "Pharisees" continues to be associated with Jews in general, negative assumptions about this ancient group have persisted and continue to be projected onto Jews in modern times. And the price for this continues to be paid.

One suggestion can prove helpful for Christians seeking to impact the Jewish-Christian relationship narrative positively: To learn about Jews and Judaism, start interacting with (or at least include) Jewish people and primary Jewish sources.

Here's a tough and graphic question from history: Would the beloved Christian Reformer Martin Luther have written the viciously anti-Semitic treatise *On the Jews and their Lies* if he had actual personal relationships with Jewish people? I want to hope that if Luther had any relationships with some Jews, it may have significantly affected his posture toward them. Many Christians are not aware Luther penned some of the vilest anti-Jewish literature we have record of.

Personal relationships with Jewish people will not lead most people to conclude they carry a religiously transmitted disease. Interactions with primary Jewish sources will not lead to the conclusion that the Pharisees, or any other mainstream Jewish groups, have ever encouraged violence.

The Weird Apostle would consider it not only strange but appalling how the group that helped shape and prepare him to be a world-class influencer has been villainized. His commitment to Jesus did not function as the antithesis to his upbringing as a Pharisee. A lot of time has been wasted through this caricature. It's time for us to wash this stereotype under the bridge.

CHAPTER 2

Paul's Weird Flash Moment

Paul was called, not converted, on the Damascus Road

THE DAMASCUS ROAD AND JIMMIE CONE ICE CREAM

I grew up in a Reform Jewish home in Burtonsville, Maryland—roughly halfway between Washington, DC, and Baltimore. Though I had a bar mitzvah, attended synagogue, and celebrated the Jewish holidays, stories from the Jewish Bible were not part of my upbringing. Even less familiar to me were stories from the New Testament. The only Damascus I knew of in my youth was the one you eventually got to if you headed northwest out of Burtonsville for about thirty-five minutes on New Hampshire Avenue.

In high school, I regularly had summer baseball games in Damascus. Even then, I was a big fan of scenic drives. The road from my old home to Damascus is a peaceful, pretty stroll through the rolling Maryland countryside. It always made me happy to go to Damascus. And my bliss multiplied when I found out about Jimmie Cone.

On one hot summer day after a game, one of the locals gave me a much-appreciated tip about a nearby landmark ice cream place that people drove from all over to visit. This fellow insisted Jimmie Cone had the best ice cream around. He was right. I can still taste those swirly soft-serve cones. And I remember the old-timey vibe, which included ordering at a walk-up window.

Jimmie Cone made delicious ice cream and it was a fun place to hang out. My friends and I enjoyed it so much that we frequented Jimmie Cone even when we didn't have baseball games. The beautiful drive and the top-shelf ice cream waiting for us made our own road to Damascus a delightful experience.

When I first heard the account of Paul's "flash moment" on the Damascus Road, I quickly discerned that it was far from glee for him. Transformative, yes. Sweet, peaceful, and delightful . . . definitely not.

PAUL'S WEIRD FLASH MOMENT

According to the New Testament, Paul's "flash moment" on the Damascus Road included a *literal* flash. Acts 9:3–9 describes his life-changing encounter:

> Now as he went on his way, he approached Damascus, and suddenly a light from heaven shone around him. And falling to the ground, he heard a voice saying to him, "Saul, Saul, why are you persecuting me?" And he said, "Who are you, Lord?"

And he said, "I am Jesus, whom you are persecuting. But rise and enter the city, and you will be told what you are to do." The men who were traveling with him stood speechless, hearing the voice but seeing no one. Saul rose from the ground, and although his eyes were opened, he saw nothing. So they led him by the hand and brought him into Damascus. And for three days he was without sight, and neither ate nor drank.

That's a bizarre encounter. If I had been in Paul's shoes, I would have been terrified to receive such a visit from someone I opposed and thought was dead. This account raises lots of questions, but one thing is clear about the mystical encounter Paul experienced at some point along the roughly 180-mile trek from Jerusalem to Damascus: It upended his life—and nothing would ever be the same.

But in what sense did Paul's life change on the Damascus Road? What do people now mean when referring to "a Damascus Road experience"? Why is this considered one of the most dramatic moments in the New Testament?

I wish I could hear your answers to these questions. I'd guess at least 90 percent of people would include a particular word in their response: "Conversion."

In the various ways people often conceptualize Paul's Damascus Road experience, "conversion" is typically the chief descriptor. That's not surprising, considering how most Bibles frame this pivotal moment. If you have a Christian Bible, try a little test on this by opening to Acts 9. You will most likely find a chapter heading that reads something like "Saul's Conversion." It is essentially an unchallenged assumption that "conversion" encapsulates the flash moment transformation when the Jewish Saul became the Christian Paul on the Damascus Road.

But let's go back to the scene of my imaginary drink with Paul:

I open my Bible to Acts 9 and say, "Hey, Paul, would you tell me more about this incredible moment?"

As Paul focuses on the page, his eyes first see the (translator-supplied) chapter heading "The Conversion of Saul."

Paul curls his eyebrows and says, "'The Conversion of Saul' . . . that's a strange way to put it. I briefly mentioned my calling in one of my letters—but I don't remember expressing what happened on the way to Damascus as a conversion."

This calling—not conversion—Paul mentioned in one of his letters refers to a passing statement he made in Galatians 1:15–17 (emphasis my own):

> But when he who had set me apart before I was born, and *who called me* by his grace, was pleased to reveal his Son to me, in order that I might preach him among the Gentiles, I did not immediately consult with anyone; nor did I go up to Jerusalem to those who were apostles before me, but I went away into Arabia, and returned again to Damascus.

This is the only place in his letters Paul mentioned his flash moment. Notice he didn't mention anything about a conversion. But he did say he was "called." In Acts 9, Luke didn't term Paul's flash moment as a conversion either. Interesting.

So why is "conversion" the typical way this moment is described? And if Paul didn't convert, what did happen on the Damascus Road? How should we describe his weird flash moment?

CALLED, BUT NOT CONVERTED

I'm guessing you're not familiar with the name Krister Stendahl. Few know of him outside the realm of the academic study of the New Testament. But Stendahl was a game changer.[27] In addition to serving as

Bishop of Stockholm and Dean of Harvard Divinity School, Stendahl was a revolutionary in the study of Paul.

In the early 1960s, Stendahl composed several papers that challenged traditional ways of understanding Paul. Scholars point to his essays "Paul among Jews and Gentiles" and "Paul and the Introspective Conscience of the West"[28] as flash moments themselves, whose jolts are still felt today. Stendahl's work was a catalyst for the modern reassessment of Paul regarding his Jewish identity and calling as an apostle to the Gentiles.

For Stendahl, a significant point that needed to be reappraised was the nature of Paul's flash moment on the Damascus Road. He was one of the first Christian thinkers in modern times to offer a corrective to the idea that Paul converted.

Stendahl's memorable point of emphasis was that Paul was called, not converted. Stendahl said:

> We must somehow recognize. . . . that Paul's message was related not to some conversion from the hopeless work righteousness of Judaism into a happy justified status as a Christian. Rather, the center of gravity of Paul's theological work is related to the fact that he knew himself to be called to be the Apostle to the Gentiles, and Apostle of the one God who is Creator of both Jews and Gentiles.[29]

Stendahl's pioneering ideas redirected how a growing number of people now view Paul's flash moment on the Damascus Road. Now, some understand Paul's epiphany was stranger than we thought. He didn't convert to a familiar form of Christianity. He remained thoroughly Jewish, albeit a Jew who held a minority viewpoint about a new stage of history that the death and resurrection of Jesus had inaugurated.

∼

DEFINING CONVERSION

Before we go any further down the Damascus Road, let's pause to define some vocabulary. By "conversion," I am referring to how an individual moves from one religious worldview and system of living to another. Conversion is typically a seismic experience involving significant changes in outlook, standards of living, and community.

Among Jews in Bible times, conversion was a contested concept.[30] Plenty of Jews welcomed converts into the fold. Others did not. But in modern Judaism, conversion is widely accepted and practiced, though it is not promoted or encouraged. In modern Christianity, "conversion" generally refers to a person's new commitment to following Jesus.

But is "conversion" an apt description of what Paul experienced on the Damascus Road? Many would say yes. After all, his name change reflected his conversion when Saul became Paul.

But is that what happened? Did Saul the Jew become Paul the Christian?

TJFKAS (THE JEW FORMERLY KNOWN AS SAUL)

Remember in the '90s when the iconic musician Prince started being referred to as the Artist Formerly Known as Prince?

At the time, Prince was unhappy about how his record label was using his name. As an act of defiance and independence, Prince wanted to be referred to by the unpronounceable Love Symbol. Because Prince assumed an unpronounceable name, people referred to him as the Artist Formerly Known as Prince. In print, some used the acronym TAFKAP.

The whole name-change thing was a weird deal. We were accustomed to calling him Prince. Even though he eventually settled his label dispute and took back his name, some of us had at least tried to use his new (not?) name because that's what he wanted to be called. It definitely made for some awkward-sounding introductions when he came on stage!

With Paul's name change, it's a different story. For most, it was a smooth and seamless transfer.

It is widely assumed that on the Damascus Road Saul the Jew was transformed into Paul the Christian. That transformation included a formal name change, which reflected his change in religions. Saul became Paul.

But unlike Prince, we don't have any sources indicating Paul's name *actually* changed. All we have is a reference in Acts 13:9 that says, "But Saul, who was also called Paul, filled with the Holy Spirit, looked intently at him . . ."

That's it. That's the big announcement that Paul's name officially changed.

Does that text say anything about a name change? I don't read it that way. Acts 13:9 simply acknowledges that the Weird Apostle had more than one name, which, for Jews then and now, is actually not so weird.

Jews in Paul's day and in ours frequently have multiple names. This is true in my case. My Hebrew name is Yerachmiel Chayim. At my synagogue, my rabbi calls me Yerachmiel. Everywhere else, I'm simply Ryan. Things were not so different with Paul.

When he was among non-Jews, Paul used his non-Jewish/ Greco-Roman name (which was actually Paulos—Paul is the English derivative). When he was with Jews, he used his Jewish name (Sh'aul— with Saul being the English derivative). This pattern is simple and easy to follow in the New Testament. Paul was just an ordinary Jewish guy in the sense that he had more than one name.

There's no name change going on here. Thus, we should not consider Paul as TJFKAS (the Jew Formerly Known as Saul)!

Perhaps you're thinking I need to simmer down on this point. Paul's name wasn't changed. "I get it already," you might be thinking. But, actually, this is a big deal.

The name-change component of Paul's story is one key pillar holding up a massive building that has largely shaped how Paul has been perceived. Most assume the apostle's name change is evidence that Saul the Jew converted to Paul the Christian. The consequences of this view of Paul's transformation have been much more significant than awkward "What do we call him now?" moments.

The "Saul the Jew converted to Paul the Christian" idea has made the apostle more familiar to Christians for many generations. But it has also augmented a misleading characterization of the nature of Paul's flash moment on the Damascus Road—and, consequently, his entire apostolic enterprise.

So what did change for Paul on the Damascus Road?

A NEW VOCATION, NOT A NEW RELIGION

On the Damascus Road, clearly, some big things changed for Paul. According to Acts 9:15, the risen Jesus commissioned Paul to carry his name "before Gentiles and kings and the children of Israel." This was a weird and radical assignment.

But this assignment was given by one Jew (Jesus) to another (Paul) to accomplish an inherently Jewish objective (share with the world that the God of Israel was the one true God).

According to the prophets who wrote the Hebrew Scriptures, an age would arrive when the God of Israel would be king over the whole earth (see Zech 14:9). The mission Jesus gave Paul signaled that the era the prophets spoke of, also referred to by Jews as the Messianic Era, was now in motion. And it was Paul's job to be the chief herald of this news to the non-Jewish world.

Paul received a new vocation on the Damascus Road. But he did not convert to a new religion.

Whether one agreed with Paul then or now that the messianic time clock had started ticking, it was a Jewish-envisioned stage of history he and his Jesus-following colleagues were convinced had begun.

According to Jewish scholar Paula Fredriksen, "[Paul's] reception of Christ turned him from antagonist to apostle. Paul refers to this as 'revelation' and as his prophetic 'call,' not as a 'conversion.'"[31]

Contrary to popular belief, no text in the New Testament supports the idea that Paul converted to another religion. Now, you might be thinking, "Hey, wait a minute, didn't Paul himself speak of his 'former life in Judaism' in his letter to the Galatians?"

Yes, he did: "For you have heard of my former life in Judaism, how I persecuted the church of God violently and tried to destroy it" (Gal 1:13).

There it is. Paul spoke of his "former life in Judaism." And his "former life in Judaism," to many, sounds like it contrasted his "current" life in Christianity. Wait just a moment, though. I have a few questions of my own:

- At that point was there an entity called "Christianity" that Paul could enter if he had exited Judaism?
- When Paul wrote Galatians, would anyone have understood or classified the Jesus movement as something outside of Judaism?
- Is there a way to understand Galatians 1:13 that does not reinforce the idea that Paul left Judaism and started or joined Christianity?

First, let's look closer at how Galatians 1:13 is typically translated. As we do, it's important to note that translations naturally reflect the biases of the translator or translation team. Historically, those involved in translating the New Testament begin with the bias that Paul converted from Judaism to Christianity. That is reflected in the English Standard Version (ESV) translation of Galatians 1:13 I just cited and in most other standard renderings.

In the ESV rendering of Galatians 1:13, translating the Greek word *pote* as "former life" fortifies the impression that Paul formerly practiced Judaism and then began practicing something else, which most assume was Christianity.

But *pote* can also be translated as "earlier." And when we do that, it sounds less like Paul was distancing himself from Judaism. This alternative rendering of Galatians 1:13 feels very different and may better capture Paul's thinking: "You have heard, no doubt, of my earlier life in Judaism . . ."[32]

Rendering Galatians 1:13 by highlighting Paul's earlier life gives the sense that Paul had a different outlook *within* Judaism at a prior point in his story. Post–Damascus Road, his outlook had changed. But it was still an outlook within Judaism. Jewish historian Mark Nanos insightfully commented on Galatians 1:13: "Interpreters traditionally have understood Paul to describe himself as no longer living in Judaism. . . . But the language Paul uses here arguably describes a certain way of living in Judaism that no longer characterizes the way he lives in Judaism now."[33]

So, to answer my previous questions, no, there was no entity called Christianity Paul could enter into—even if he wanted to depart from Judaism. When Paul wrote Galatians, the Jesus movement was expanding beyond Jewish borders. But it was still a movement classified as a Jewish development—by both Jews and non-Jews. While Galatians 1:13 spoke of Paul's "former life in Judaism," it could refer to an earlier phase of Paul's life in Judaism, as opposed to a life (or religion) he had abandoned.

Jesus tasked Paul to carry a message of light and redemption to the Gentiles. It was a new chapter for him. A new calling. A new vocation. But not a new religion.

However, there is a caveat I'd like to throw in the mix regarding Paul, the Damascus Road, and the term "conversion." While Paul did not switch from one religion to another, is there any sense in which we can say Paul experienced a conversion as a result of his weird flash moment? Maybe so.

A CONVERSION CAVEAT

Did Paul experience a conversion on the Damascus Road? Well, I'll give you a good Jewish answer to my question.

No . . . and yes.

No, Paul did not experience a conversion on the Damascus Road—if we are referring to a *macro* conversion in which Paul departed from Judaism and began to form a new religion that would eventually be called Christianity.

I can hear some of you again yelling for me to pump the brakes: "Not so fast. Didn't Paul negate the Torah, disparage circumcision, and point out the emptiness of Judaism? Is that not a conversion?"

I hear you. Yes, those things are indeed attributed to Paul. Bear with me—we'll address that in chapter 6. And we need to talk about it, because the direction of the wind is changing about how Paul is understood not only as a Jew but also about his fidelity in those ideas regarding the Torah, circumcision, and Judaism.

For now, before we pivot away from the conversion topic as it relates to Paul, I will continue to nuance this a bit.

There is a sense that we can conceptualize Paul experiencing a micro-conversion.

When he began his journey to Damascus, Paul opposed the Jesus movement, and there is no evidence that he was in any way persuaded that the Messianic Era, the kingdom of God, or the end of the age that the Jewish prophets had spoken of had begun. As a Pharisee, Paul likely expected those things to happen in the future. Messianic expectations were standard for Pharisees like Paul because they upheld the writings of the Hebrew prophets, which pointed to a future, global end-times redemption. But for pre–Damascus Road Paul, that time had not yet come.

However, on the Damascus Road, something dramatic happened to Paul. He believed the prophetic hopes within Judaism were now in motion. Thus, I think it is accurate to describe Paul's experience as a type of conversion—but it was a conversion *within* Judaism pertaining to *time*.

Paul was persuaded that the resurrection of Jesus launched a new era for the Jewish people. A more theological way of framing this is that Paul believed Judaism had shifted into an apocalyptic, eschatological, messianic, and prophetic phase.

So, in relation to time and *within Judaism*, it's fair to say Paul experienced a type of conversion. Again, here's a helpful statement from Fredriksen: "True to his temperament, Paul went all in, from one form of Jewishness to another: apocalyptic, pneumatic, messianic, and with a particularly Pharisaic emphasis on resurrection . . ."[34]

So, yes, Paul's weird flash moment on the Damascus Road resulted in a dramatic change. Most of his Jewish brethren thought he was out of his mind to proclaim such things as he was. But Paul was proclaiming *Jewish things* he believed should now extend to the rest of the world. And that never changed until the day he died.

HOW DOES PAUL'S WEIRD FLASH MOMENT CHANGE THE GAME?

Rethinking and reframing Paul's weird flash moment as a calling, rather than a conversion, is a game-changing idea that is currently in motion. It's no longer universally accepted that Saul the Jew became Paul the Christian in a flash on the Damascus Road.

Thinkers across the Jewish, Christian, and academic spectrums are making Paul's Damascus Road flash moment weird—again. A range of voices are working to recast Paul's assumed conversion story in favor of a less familiar but more historically probable account that emphasizes his calling. One such voice is Isaac Oliver, a Jewish scholar specializing in reading the New Testament, Luke and Acts in particular, as Jewish texts. Oliver agrees using "conversion" to describe Paul's story is problematic. He writes:

[Paul] moving from believing in the resurrection to believing in its confirmation does not constitute a "conversion" story. . . . The term "conversion," therefore, seems unsuitable for appreciating Luke's Jewish portrait of Paul. . . . All three accounts in Acts about Paul's Damascus experience, then, are set within the framework of calling: Paul is a chosen instrument, who has been appointed and sent forth to proclaim the good tidings about Jesus's lordship and resurrection.[35]

Another is David Claussen, a historian who specializes in Christian origins. He also thinks Paul's origin as an apostle should be reconsidered, writing:

Paul understood his encounter with Christ as a vocational calling rather than a religious "conversion" if by conversion we mean abandoning one religious tradition for another. . . . Paul seemed to understand that he, like Jeremiah, was predestined to fulfill a special calling, in his case one that focused on preaching Christ to the gentiles. But note what the calling did not include. His calling was not to forsake his religious heritage. It was not to preach Christ to Jews. It was not to turn gentiles into Jews. It had a very limited objective with profound consequences.[36]

Indeed, Paul's calling had profound consequences that would eventually contribute to shaping the world as we know it. Yes, rethinking his Damascus Road flash moment as a calling rather than a conversion may feel weird. Doing so, however, not only presents a more feasible portrait of Paul, but it can also have profound implications as we consider the modern relationship between Christians and Jews.

~

GAME-CHANGING ACTION

The standard narrative that Paul converted from Judaism to Christianity on the Damascus Road has helped draw a clear line of distinction and, all too often, bitter contention between Christians and Jews. Because Christians and Jews disagree about the identity of Jesus and other foundational ideas, the gradual development of a border between the two groups was not only inevitable but healthy. However, it was not inevitable (or healthy) that the perimeters would feature thick walls, armed guards, and hostile relations.

Paul's so-called conversion from Judaism to Christianity is not the sole cause for the fortification between the now-distinct religions. However, the "Saul converted to Paul on the Damascus Road" narrative sits at the bedrock level of the rampart built long ago that still separates Jews and Christians.

Suppose you are Jewish and embrace the prevailing viewpoint that Paul converted to Christianity because he saw Judaism as a failure. In that case, it creates the impression that one of your former family members defected and betrayed his people in pursuit of a superior option. That is the way most Jews see Paul. Thus, understandably, most Jews don't get the warm fuzzies when Paul comes up.

As a Christian, if your mindset is that one of your leading players left Judaism to convert to Christianity, it bolsters an outlook that views Christianity as superseding Judaism and the Christian Church replacing the Jewish people.

And each of these angles, which do indeed reflect the way Jews and Christians have largely understood each other for the past two thousand years, has harvested endless hostility. But imagine how relations might improve between Christians and Jews if these assumptions were reconsidered.

I am not suggesting we minimize the fundamental differences between Christians and Jews. The disagreement about Jesus and all that flows from that is a big deal. But let's play the "what if" game for a moment.

What if Christians saw Paul as a Jewish messenger who was called to herald redemption for non-Jews while never departing Judaism? Well, that would represent a massive paradigm shift for Christians that would positively affect their relationships with Jews. If Paul continued respecting and practicing Judaism *as an apostle*, that would imply that Christians should also embrace the immense ongoing validity and value of Judaism.

What if Jews upheld that Paul continued to love and practice Judaism and was dedicated first and foremost to expanding the family of God to include non-Jews? Actually, there are such Jews. Michael Wyschogrod, an Orthodox Jewish philosopher and theologian who had a deep interest in Jewish-Christian relations, said, "There is a form of [Pauline] Christianity that does not intend to replace Israel as the people of God but join it as adopted sons and daughters in the household of God. The existence of this Christianity has helped me shape a Jewish identity that can live in deep appreciation of this new Christianity."[37]

Yes, there is an emerging form of Christianity that does *not* include a Paul who was dedicated to replacing Israel and the Jewish people. At the center of this development is the understanding that Paul believed his mission included an invitation for non-Jews to join the household of God, not a new religion. Hopefully, this form of Christianity will continue to grow, and as a result, more Jews can appreciate it like Wyschogrod.

Paul's weird flash moment on the Damascus Road was certainly definitive. It changed not only his life, but history too.

Yet some of Paul's history needs to be rethought. Doing so will move us closer to the authentic Weird Apostle. And it will move us further down the road of positive relations between Christians and Jews.

CHAPTER 3

Paul's Weird Mission

*Paul's mission that the Jewish God is the God of all was
disruptive and dangerous*

DID HE REALLY ASK ME THAT?

Surprisingly, I'm starting to feel more comfortable with him.
He is opening up. And I am loving it! But then he asks a totally
unexpected question.

"Ryan," Paul says with a relaxed but serious expression, "have you ever been to prison?"

Why in the world would Paul ask me this? Whatever ease I am beginning to feel departs. I straighten up, slowly grab my glass, and raise it near to take a sip.

"No, Paul, I've never been to prison." I pause. "But I came real close."

CAMDEN YARDS AND SOME BOYS ON A MISSION

I do not have a criminal record. And I've never been arrested. But I've been close. Very close.

It was a winter night in 1992. I don't know if the moon was full, or if some other phenomenon could explain why a group of us teenagers—a future doctor, lawyer, professional baseball manager, religious educator, and highly successful entrepreneur—came up with such a crazy, screwball, illegal idea. But it was an idea that became a weird and wild mission.

The occasion for us being together was Patrick's birthday. I'm unsure who devised the plan, but we were all in. And perhaps the only clear part of our thinking was this: We were teenagers with a mission to make it an unforgettable night. And somehow, we would get onto the field at Oriole Park at Camden Yards in Baltimore, Maryland.

OUR WAIT WAS OVER

My friends and I grew up as big Baltimore Orioles fans. Before we were teenagers, we attended ball games at the old Memorial Stadium on Thirty-Third Street. I have great memories from "the old stadium."

I remember the legendary Wild Bill Hagy in Section 34, who used to whip the upper deck into a frenzy and lead us in the O-R-I-O-L-E-S chant. To this day, when possible, my family still sits on the third base side at ballgames because that's what we did in the old stadium. Why the third base side? Because my mom's favorite player growing up was the Orioles' third baseman, Brooks Robinson, and she always sat on the third base side to be close to Brooksie. It's funny how traditions start.

When the Orioles announced in the late 1980s that they would build a new downtown stadium close to the harbor, baseball fans in the area had mixed feelings about saying goodbye to Memorial Stadium. We had so many memories there. But the new stadium sounded fantastic. And as big O's fans, we couldn't wait to see it. So, on that cold night in 1992, my friends and I decided we had waited long enough.

Adding to our motivation to get inside the still-under-construction Camden Yards was that we were all baseball players. And we were good. The friends on this mission helped Paint Branch High School win back-to-back Maryland state championships in the early '90s. So, we were used to operating together. It's just that, usually, our efforts were lawful.

But that night, our quest did not include a consideration of how our lives might be disrupted if our mission went awry. We were all gas and no brakes.

When we arrived at Camden Yards, we found the stadium nearly completed. However, there were still construction fences in place. Being a smart posse, we smelled an opportunity. We found an opening at the bottom of one of the fences within minutes. With ease, we made our way under.

We were in. We were really inside Oriole Park at Camden Yards.

Immediately, we sprinted past what would become a concessions area and made our way straight for the baseball field. The field looked green and beautiful. The lighting was minimal, but there was plenty enough for us to see. The five of us ran around the field like wild banshees. We didn't have baseball equipment. And we didn't need it. We simulated diving catches, stolen bases, and home runs.

Nobody was there but us. But we could imagine the excitement of what it would feel like with fifty thousand fans cheering in the seats around us. Our energy was overflowing. What a rush.

Our fun led us into the third base dugout, where we exchanged high fives and sat on the benches as if we had just finished a game. Our smiles could not have been bigger. For a moment, we felt like major leaguers.

But in an instant, we went from major leaguers to major trouble.

Beyond the right field wall, we saw two flashlights held by what looked like two uniformed officers. And they were running in our direction.

So, what did we do? We did what most teenagers on a reckless mission do.

We ran.

THE FAMOUS "PAPERWORK" LINE

The five teenagers fleeing from security guards had not gotten into one bit of *serious* trouble up to this point in our lives. We were good kids, earned good grades, and had solid values. We were way out of our element in this caper. But we were still full throttle. And still running.

When we reached the concourse, we agreed to hide in one of the bathrooms until the coast was clear. How would we know the coast was clear? We had no good answer. We waited there for about ten minutes. Then we decided to make a run for it—again.

As we rounded our way around the concourse, guess who met us?

I'll never forget the first question from the security guards. "Y'all been drinkin' over at Pickles Pub?"

Pickles Pub? No, we had not been to Pickles. But I remember thinking we were definitely in one.

The guards told us they were going to take us downtown and book us for trespassing. I could not imagine what my parents were going to think.

As they escorted us to the area close to where we entered, one guard looked at the other and said, "You feel like doin' the paperwork on this one?" The other one said, "Nah, not really." They then scolded us and told us they better not see us in there again. We thanked them profusely and swiftly made our way out of the stadium.

We all agreed the next time we visited Camden Yards, we would do so with an admission ticket.

A DIFFERENT KIND OF DISTURBANCE

I've told that story about the Camden Yards mission many times. The great thing about this tale is that it requires no embellishment. It really happened that way.

But a few times, I've wondered what would have happened if the guards *did* have us arrested and taken downtown. It probably wouldn't have upended our lives permanently, but it certainly would have destabilized them. As star athletes on a high-profile high school baseball team, our escapade could have drawn some media attention, for one.

But when it comes to the instability caused by Paul's mission, it's a whole different ball game.

On the Damascus Road, Paul received a calling that would lead to not just one crazy night, but to a mission that would create instability and turmoil for the rest of his life—and plenty of arrests and imprisonments (see 2 Cor 11:23).

MY ANSWER

Paul smiles as I recount the break-in at Camden Yards. I think the Weird Apostle inclines toward edgy stories.

"So, no, Paul, I have never been arrested or imprisoned. But I'm aware you were many times. Along that line, can I ask you a question?" He nods agreeably. "All those imprisonments, beatings, and everything you endured . . . was it worth it? Would you do it again?"

Prefaced with a quick, tender smile, Paul's initial response is one word: "Absolutely."

I can tell there is more, but he is silent for a moment. Then he says, "The times in prison were worth it because the mission was worth it—no question about it. But, Ryan, as you've already noted, there are some big misunderstandings about what my mission was really about. Big misunderstandings."

Paul's mission rocked his world and continues to shake the globe to this day. It's a mission he was willing to be repeatedly arrested and imprisoned for. And it's a mission that is widely misunderstood.

HOW WOULD YOU SUMMARIZE PAUL'S MISSION?

If you can't already tell, I'm a people person. And I love to ask questions. That's why I have questions peppered throughout this book. I wish I could hear your answers to them.

One can learn a lot by being a persistent question-asker. Just this morning, I had coffee with a leadership coach at my local chamber of commerce. I asked her, "What is a leadership idea that changes the game?" Wow, did she come alive with that question. Her passion oozed.

When I sit across from someone with passion, it almost doesn't matter what they are talking about. Their passion makes me lean forward.

Okay, I'm digressing . . . sort of. That was a long intro to an important question I want to ask. And if you don't have an answer, that's fine. But here goes:

How would you summarize Paul's mission?

I have had countless conversations with Christians and Jews about Paul for several decades. And though Paul is notoriously difficult to understand, there is a surprisingly common and straightforward answer to my question above.

Paul's mission was to start Christianity.

Many will nuance this viewpoint with additional or modified statements, such as:

- "Of course, Jesus was the founder of Christianity. But Paul was the first missionary who aimed to spread Christianity around the world."
- "Well, Christianity as a religion didn't exist yet in Paul's day. But Paul clarified that you don't have to keep the law to be a Christian. It's all about Jesus. And that was a big change that led to what became Christianity."
- "Paul started it all by planting churches throughout the Middle East during his missionary journeys. This is how Christianity started."

These ideas about Paul's mission are familiar to many people. My guess is you hold some form of these viewpoints, or have at least heard them before.

But I'd like to challenge these ideas. These ideas largely obscure what Paul's mission was all about. Paul's mission did not include planting churches or starting a new religion called Christianity—at least not in the familiar sense of these terms. So, if Paul didn't start Christianity and he didn't plant churches, what *was* Paul's weird, game-changing mission? If I had to summarize it in one line, it would be this:

Paul's mission was to persuade the non-Jewish nations of the world (Gentiles) to abandon their gods and give exclusive allegiance to the God of Israel because Jesus's death and resurrection inaugurated the new utopian era foretold by the Jewish prophets.

But we need to press in further, and then we'll do our best to flesh out Paul's weird mission. Here we go:

Paul's mission was to bring good news to non-Jews that the time had come to turn from their native gods, idols, and pagan practices and give singular worship to the God of Abraham, Isaac, and Jacob. The one true God of the Jews was the God of all. And because of Jesus's redeeming death and resurrection, and in accord with the expectations of the Jewish prophets, God's spirit was working in new ways to transform unholy pagans into holy men and women who could become members in equal standing within Abraham's family, the family of God. This mission included non-Jews forsaking all devotion to the gods and acculturating to a Jesus-centered, Torah-based way of life alongside Jews, while maintaining their unique destiny and identities as members of the nations.

This is a huge point of this book. And here's what we need to grapple with next: Paul's mission, as weird as they come, was nothing short of scandalous. And that was a big problem for Jewish people and for the non-Jews to whom he was called to reach.

∽

AN OUTRAGEOUS, DANGEROUS, AND
PROBLEMATIC MISSION

It was outrageous for a Jewish man like Paul to declare that his mission from God was to persuade non-Jews to abandon their (many) gods and give singular allegiance to the God of the Jews.

Where we currently stand, we don't flinch at non-Jews embracing only one God. However, in Paul's day, that was a categorical impossibility. In the era the New Testament was forming, to be *ta ethne* (Greek for "the nations" or "Gentile") was to be polytheistic—to worship many gods.

For non-Jews in the Greco-Roman world, worshipping the gods was not something you decided to do. In Paul's time, it was an inherited component of one's ethnicity. Pagan veneration was as natural to everyday life as eating and making a living. Paula Fredriksen, in her excellent book *The Pagan's Apostle*, elegantly describes this interwovenness:

> The gods were everywhere, not only in public and private buildings of ancient municipalities, but also on insignia of office, on military standards, in solemn oaths and contracts, in vernacular benedictions and exclamations, and all throughout the curriculum of the educated. It was impossible to live in a Greco-Roman city without living with its gods.[38]

But Paul was persuaded a new day had arrived that upended core social institutions and identities. As the apostle to the Gentiles, his mission represented a new era in which *ta ethne* should stop honoring their local gods and worship the Jewish God alone. For Paul, such upheaval was befitting of the new stage of history inaugurated by Jesus's resurrection and in accord with the expectations of the Jewish prophets of old.

But for those who did not view Jesus and the times as Paul did, his mission didn't just come across as weird. It was downright dangerous, representing a major disruption to the status quo for Jews and non-Jews.

PAUL'S WEIRD MISSION WAS A JEWISH PROBLEM

Paul's Damascus Road experience was clearly a weird encounter, as we noted in the previous chapter. To be stopped in your tracks by a supposedly dead Jewish revolutionary is strange. But resurrections and visitations from dead charismatic leaders are not unprecedented in Judaism.

To this day, various sects of Judaism claim to receive messages from deceased leaders.[39] Such visits are controversial and looked at with skepticism by some Jews. But they do not set off community-wide alarm bells.

Paul would have received his share of sideways glances had he merely claimed to witness Jesus in a resurrected body. But the specific directive Paul claimed to receive from the man he previously thought was dead threatened the well-being of Jews across the Roman Empire.

Jews had legitimate concerns that Paul's mission would destabilize their delicate relationship with the Greco-Roman authorities that governed the territories they lived in, which Paul was now targeting.

JEWS AND ROME: A FRAGILE DYNAMIC

Rome had mixed feelings about Jews and their way of life in Paul's time. On the one hand, they granted Jews throughout their broad empire—and in Israel—significant freedom to live and worship according to their ancient customs. Unlike their non-Jewish neighbors, Jews were not obligated to offer obeisance to the pantheon of Greco-Roman gods. This massively important exemption was a unique privilege for Jews.

However, the Jewish exemption was likely a dynamic many Romans were less than enthusiastic about. The Jewish worship of their God alone was more so a tolerated practice. From a Roman perspective, Jews were atheists. That idea probably has a strange ring to it.

How could Jews, with their deep devotion to the God of the Bible, be considered atheists?

From a Greco-Roman standpoint, worshipping only one god and being aniconic (having no icons, representations, and images in their worship expressions) was equivalent to being "a" (against) "theistic" (belief in the existence of, in the case of non-Jews in Paul's time, the gods). In modern times, being an atheist is an acceptable social position. In Paul's day, this label was far from benign.

Jews being categorized as atheists included a dangerous stigma. Declining to worship and appease the many gods who were deeply involved in day-to-day affairs was akin to rejecting the entire order that kept the cosmos and everyday life intact. Jews were peculiar in this regard, standing out wherever they lived, especially in Roman cities outside Israel. Thus, Jews in the Roman Empire knew their dispensation to abstain from the pagan cult was brittle and needed to be delicately protected.

Thus, for Jews, there was a clear, though not easy, formula to keep themselves safe as residents of the Roman Empire: Stay quiet, don't cause trouble, try to get along with the Roman authorities—and don't mess with the Romans' worship of their gods.

Yes, a time would come, according to the Jewish Bible,[40] when non-Jews would abandon their gods and worship the Jewish God alone. But that time had not yet come.

Enter Paul. Can you smell the trouble?

(UPENDING) THE GRECO-ROMAN FORMULA FOR STAYING SAFE AND BLESSED

In the Greco-Roman world Paul lived in, non-Jews also had a formula for keeping their families and cities safe and blessed: Keep the gods happy.

The gods were happy when everyone did their part to offer the appropriate homage. Happy gods protected cities from earthquakes, sickness, and invasions. Satisfied deities were the ultimate defense mechanism in an age when peril was always around the corner.

Again, as rare exceptions, Jews in Paul's day were not required to invoke the gods. But it was without question that all non-Jewish Greco-Roman citizens were expected to participate in the standard acts of veneration exercised in all aspects of life. It was this elemental cultural norm that Paul was determined to change because, in his mind, the new, prophetic era Jesus had initiated called for it. And the inevitable collision between Paul and this intrinsic component of Greco-Roman society set the Jewish community on edge.

The math was clear for the Jewish community: Paul's mission was hazardous. But to Paul, the times required whatever backlash might result from his mission. He was persuaded that Jesus's resurrection inaugurated the age that the prophets of Israel longed for. Prophetic texts such as Zechariah 14:9 shaped the hopes and expectations of Jews like Paul: "And the Lord will be king over all the earth. On that day the Lord will be one and his name one."

For Paul, Zechariah's vision was in motion—now. His mission compelled him to declare that the prophetic time clock had started ticking. This meant the hour had come for non-Jews to turn away from idols and gods and offer exclusive fidelity to the God of the Jews—whom Paul believed was the one, true God for all people. As he stated in his letter to the Romans, "Or is God the God of Jews only? Is he not the God of Gentiles also? Yes, of Gentiles also, since God is one" (Rom 3:29–30).

Paul's mission represented an unprecedented Jewish approach to engaging Gentiles that escalated the stakes for all involved.

PAUL'S MISSION RAISED THE BAR FOR NON-JEWS

To understand just how radical and destabilizing Paul's mission was, we need to discuss the engagement that non-Jews had with

Jews and Judaism before and during Paul's time. The non-Jews who embraced Paul's Jewish-oriented, Jesus-centered mission were not the first Gentiles to be drawn to the Jewish God and way of life. The New Testament and other early Christian sources reference a mysterious, loose category of people called god-fearers. These were non-Jews who had varying levels of engagement in Judaism and synagogue life.

The New Testament mentions god-fearers both in Israel and in the diaspora—which, from a Jewish standpoint, refers to areas outside Israel. A prominent New Testament example of a non-Jewish god-fearer is Cornelius. Acts 10:1–2 describes him as "a centurion of what was known as the Italian Cohort, a devout man who feared God with all his household."

While god-fearers positively engaged with the Jewish community and synagogue life, they did not convert fully to Judaism. And no sources outline or preserve a systematic program for god-fearers to adhere to. Contrary to what many people envision, being a god-fearer was not a formal category with clear parameters.

At this point, I know some of you may be wondering, "What about the Noahide Laws? Wouldn't the Jewish community have expected god-fearers to keep these laws?"

Well, it's hard to say. I'll explain.

WHAT ABOUT THE NOAHIDE LAWS?

You are not alone if you haven't heard of the Noahide Laws. Many people are unfamiliar with these seven commandments mentioned in post-New-Testament-era rabbinic literature. The rabbis believed these seven laws were incumbent upon all of humanity. In other words, sources from the rabbinic era, which were produced after the New Testament period, held up the Noahide Laws as standards for non-Jews to maintain.

Positively, the Noahide Laws included establishing courts of justice. Negatively, these laws included prohibitions on illicit sexual relationships, theft, and, very importantly, idolatry. However, there are two reasons why I don't think the Jewish community in Paul's time expected god-fearers to keep the Noahide Laws.

First, while these laws have a basis in the Torah, they were not codified by the rabbis until Talmudic times—several hundred years after Paul. So, we don't have evidence of the Noahide Laws being a distinguishable concept in Paul's time that the Jewish community could appeal to as a code for god-fearers to follow.

Second, if some early form of the Noahide Laws circulated orally during Paul's time, Jews had good reasons *not* to impose the Noahide Laws on god-fearers for fear of the backlash that would come from the idolatry prohibition. Jews knew undermining Gentile fealty to the gods had treacherous implications.

So, yes, in Paul's time, some non-Jews expressed a positive interest in Jews, Judaism, and synagogue life. But, importantly, there was no expectation from the Jewish community that Gentile god-fearers would discontinue their allegiance to the gods.

Now, some Jews expected Gentiles would restrict their worship to the Jewish God *when the Messiah arrived*. For most first-century Jews, that time had not yet arrived. After his Damascus Road experience, Paul was persuaded otherwise.

As the "pagan's apostle," Paul was on a mission to proclaim that Jesus's resurrection catalyzed the time for non-Jews to join the family of Abraham and give exclusive worship to Abraham's God. That meant it was no longer acceptable for them to offer devotion to the Greco-Roman pantheon of gods.

THERE WAS GOOD REASON TO SWEAT

Can you feel the tension? As Jewish communities around the Roman Empire gained an understanding of Paul's mission to non-Jews, they knew they had a big problem on their hands. Paul was one of their own. And though many Jews did not share his view of Jesus, no Jew would argue that he was circulating a definitively Jewish message.

Paul had to be stopped.

The strong opposition Paul faced from his fellow Jews was not directly because he upheld Jesus as the Jewish Messiah. Rather, opposition from Jews arose from their concern that Paul's mission to non-Jews would generate a reprisal from the Roman authorities. And according to the book of Acts, this is exactly what happened.

Acts 19:23–27 offers insight into the problems Paul caused in the Roman city of Ephesus and wherever he traveled:

> About that time there arose no little disturbance concerning the Way. For a man named Demetrius, a silversmith, who made silver shrines of Artemis, brought no little business to the craftsmen. These he gathered together, with the workmen in similar trades, and said, "Men, you know that from this business we have our wealth. And you see and hear that not only in Ephesus but in almost all of Asia this Paul has persuaded and turned away a great many people, saying that gods made with hands are not gods. And there is danger not only that this trade of ours may come into disrepute but also that the temple of the great goddess Artemis may be counted as nothing, and that she may even be deposed from her magnificence, she whom all Asia and the world worship."

Clearly, the non-Jews in Ephesus were concerned about the results of Paul's mission. Remember, from a Greco-Roman perspective, angering the gods led to negative consequences within the given god's domain. And as this account from Acts notes, fewer Gentiles worshipping the gods also affected local businesses whose trades depended upon the pagan cults. This is the last thing the Jewish community wanted to be associated with. They were being drawn into a fiasco because of Paul.

Acts 19:32–34 continues describing the account in Ephesus, and it's not good for the Jews there:

> Now some cried out one thing, some another, for the assembly was in confusion, and most of them did not know why they had come together. Some of the crowd prompted Alexander, whom the Jews had put forward. And Alexander, motioning with his hand, wanted to make a defense to the crowd. But when they recognized that he was a Jew, for about two hours they all cried out with one voice, "Great is Artemis of the Ephesians!"

Again, there was no Christianity or local network of distinctly identifiable Christian churches for the Jewish community to pin Paul to. The Christ-following assemblies that did exist were likely still synagogue subgroups. It sounds weird, and I'm planning to dig more into this in my next book, but churches at this time were part of the broader network of synagogues. Thus, the Gentile authorities looked to Jewish leaders to quell the mayhem Paul was causing.

The Jewish community wanted nothing to do with this mess, but Paul was one of theirs, so they were drawn into the uproar that followed apparently wherever he went. This is why Paul wrote in one of his letters that the Jewish community disciplined him frequently and harshly: "Five times I received at the hands of the Jews the forty lashes less one. Three times I was beaten with rods. Once I was stoned" (2 Cor 11:24–25).

Institutions and organizations are responsible for disciplining those within their community who don't follow the rules. Paul was a representative of the Jewish community and remained organically part of the synagogue realm. Thus, his actions affected Jews everywhere. And, understandably, on numerous occasions, the Jewish community tried to beat this mission out of the Weird Apostle.

Merely being a public advocate for a messianic candidate would not justify, and likely would not have produced, such severe responses from the Jewish community. Being the catalyst for citywide distur-bances that produced peril for the Jewish community would.

This is why Jews viewed Paul's mission as not only weird, but also deadly.

PAUL'S WEIRD MISSION WAS A GENTILE PROBLEM

Paul's mission also had potentially fatal consequences from a Gentile perspective. Although non-Jewish worldviews varied widely in the ancient world, keeping the gods happy was preeminent across the geographical and cultural landscape. People did their part to offer the proper worship and obeisance to those gods who presided over their given location.

So, it's not hard to imagine why Paul experienced resistance when he arrived in a new region proclaiming his gospel. If his message was confined to the claim that the God of the Jews was offering forgive-ness to all of humanity through Jesus, his mission would still have been unwelcome by many. A Jewish message of forgiveness to Gentiles would sound odd, or even arrogant, to lots of folks.

Paul's mission went much further. The Weird Apostle drove deep into the core of Greco-Roman existence. Those who embraced his message could not merely add Jesus to their congested mix of divine loyalties. Paul said that if one expressed *pistis* (Greek for "faith" or "alle-giance") to the Jewish God because of and through Jesus, all other gods had to go. Paul said this succinctly and clearly in a letter to a non-Jewish community of Jesus's followers in the city of Corinth:

> Therefore, as to the eating of food offered to idols, we know that "an idol has no real existence," and that "there is no God but one." For although there may be so-called gods in heaven or on earth—as indeed there are many "gods" and many "lords"—yet for us there is one God, the Father, from whom are all things

and for whom we exist, and one Lord, Jesus Christ, through whom are all things and through whom we exist. (1 Cor 8:4–6)

It is impossible for us to comprehend how weird, difficult, and dangerous such a statement would sound to a first-century resident of a city like Corinth. If you were not persuaded by Paul's message about Jesus, then you would have good reason to be wary of your friends, family, or neighbors who did.

What about keeping the city safe? What about keeping your family safe? What about ensuring calamity doesn't strike? These were the questions and concerns of a resident of Corinth, Thessalonica, or Athens regarding a path (and a community) that no longer included satisfying the gods.

THE MASSIVE STRAIN FOR "PAUL'S GENTILES"

If you were a Gentile persuaded by Paul's message, especially in the first few generations of the Jesus movement, you were in a tenuous social position. Paul unequivocally forbade his Gentiles from worshipping the gods. In his letter to the Galatians, he said:

Formerly, when you did not know God, you were enslaved to those that by nature are not gods. But now that you have come to know God, or rather to be known by God, how can you turn back again to the weak and worthless elementary principles of the world, whose slaves you want to be once more? (Gal 4:8–9)

When Paul said "the weak and worthless elementary principles of the world," read that as "worshipping the gods." Paul said non-Jews who had embraced Christ could not do that anymore. Based on our discussion, you can envision how problematic this would be. It would not take long to experience alienation and perhaps persecution from people you once enjoyed harmony with. Not only would you appear withdrawn when you didn't participate in day-to-day pagan conventions, but you would be a natural target when small or large disasters struck. Can you imagine the strain?

It is these challenges and more that lead me to think it was non-Jewish Christ-followers, as opposed to Jewish ones, who had much more to lose by becoming Jesus's followers in Paul's time and in the decades that followed.

It is frequently assumed that *Jewish* Christ-followers were the ones who faced the most opposition in the early generations of the Jesus movement. And there's no question that they faced troubles for following Jesus also.

But for Jews, following Jesus did not include a thorough deconstruction and reconstruction of their worldview and lifestyle. Jewish Christ-followers embraced a minority viewpoint, but it was still a concept and movement within Judaism in Paul's time.

For non-Jews, following Jesus included a comprehensive personal and social reformation that led to tension in ways that are difficult for us to fathom.

According to Paul, it was all worth it. The God of Israel was on the move in unprecedented ways. Jesus was God's appointed agent of redemption. He was the "light for the Gentiles" who would bring salvation to the ends of the earth that the prophet Isaiah spoke of (Isa 49:5–6). Whatever disruption and loss Paul's Gentiles experienced paled in comparison to the rewards and blessings that would soon come when Jesus returned and God was king over all the earth.

HOW DOES PAUL'S WEIRD MISSION CHANGE THE GAME?

My kids find it humorous that during this season of writing *The Weird Apostle*, I am watching the Netflix series *Outer Banks*. My kids and I are close, so they feel safe teasing me. I am thankful for that.

Outer Banks is not a series I would normally choose to watch, but my wife recently asked me to watch it with her. I was reluctant to commit to a series about a bunch of teenagers on a treasure hunt, but once we started, I got sucked in. I enjoy the characters and the storyline keeps me on my toes. So, yes, I'm a fan of *Outer Banks*. The kids can poke fun at me all they want—I'm enjoying it. And it's good to make my sweetheart happy by watching it with her!

Season two of *Outer Banks* revolves around "the Pogues" contending with false criminal accusations pinned on their group leader and the main character, John B. John B. is on the run for most of the season, evading various foes and trying to prove his innocence. As it typically goes on the screen, the truth comes forth and clears John B.'s name. With a few plot twists over several forty-five-minute episodes, the final episode of the season sets the story straight.

However, when it comes to the prevailing narrative regarding Paul's mission, it's a different story. Assumptions and accusations about his mission continue to distort his record. And it will take much more than forty-five minutes to clear his name.

However, the fog is beginning to lift.

PAUL, THE FOUNDER OF CHRISTIANITY?

Over the past two thousand years, it has been mostly uncontested among Christians and Jews that Paul's mission was centered on starting a new religion we call Christianity. For Christians, this has been an assumption. For Jews, it has been an accusation.

Christians are proud and relieved that Paul took a stand and founded a religion and network of churches that exchanged the legalism of Judaism for the grace of Christianity.

For Jews, Paul is accused of abandoning his people and his faith and pursuing an easier law/Torah-free path that would gain him and his mission far greater acceptance.

Foundational ideas frequently attributed to Paul's mission, these familiar assumptions and accusations make for a congruous history that is neatly indexed in our history books, in doctrinal statements, and in our minds.

However, these assumptions and accusations do not accurately represent Paul or his mission. Paul's mission was not to start Christianity. And he didn't establish Christian churches as we know them. The excellent scholar of early Christianity Dr. John Gager expresses this clearly:

> Did Paul really make early Christianity? Of course not. . . . Not only did Paul not make early Christianity, he had no conception of what we call Christianity. . . . His goal was to bring Gentile believers in Jesus Christ into the eschatological [end-times] people of God, not to annul the Law for Jews. . . . What we call Christianity is not just post-Pauline; it is un-Pauline.[41]

Those are game-changing words from Gager. Paul's mission was to persuade the world that the Jewish God is the God of all people and nations. Because of Jesus's death and resurrection, Paul believed the time had come for Gentiles to abandon their gods and follow the God of Israel alone. That allegiance included organizing one's outlook and life according to the principles of the Jewish Torah, as appropriately applied to non-Jews. This was Paul's mission.

His mission did not include founding a Jesus-centered, law-free church that superseded Judaism and replaced it as the true, authentic, Spirit-infused religion. Paul's later interpreters believed this to be his mission. But such a mission would have been foreign to Paul.

∼

WHO IS THE REAL WEIRDO IN THIS CONVERSATION?

Paul's mission also did not include planting churches. At this point, some of you are probably thinking Ryan Lambert is the real weird one here. "What in the world do you mean Paul didn't plant churches? Of course he planted churches—and we have Paul's letters and the book of Acts to prove it!" I hear you. So, let's sort this out.

Paul's mission definitely included planting Christ-centered communities. But in Paul's time, these churches were very different from what churches became in the decades and centuries that followed Paul.

In Paul's day, churches (*ekklesiae* in Greek) were still connected to the synagogue. As the Pauline scholar Mark Nanos[42] has said for decades, ekklesiae were actually "synagogue subgroups." Later, yes, churches as we have come to know them have disconnected from the synagogue. But in Paul's day, they were umbilically connected to each other.

Where else would Paul's Gentiles have accessed the Jewish Scriptures he instructed them to learn? Where else would they have learned about the God of Abraham? Where else would they have received instruction in the principles of Torah that were appropriate for them to follow as non-Jews engaged in a Jewish messianic movement?

There was one place Paul's Gentiles could access such resources and teaching that his letters obliged them to pursue: synagogues. Oddly enough, in Paul's day, to go to church was to go to the synagogue. In other words, Paul's ekklesiae were Christ-centered assemblies that gathered within the orbit of synagogue life.

We know things changed drastically in the generations after Paul's time. Church became something "other" in relation to Jews and Judaism. Synagogue and church became separate. But it's important to understand that Paul had no idea such a split would occur.

Paul's weird mission created massive problems for both Jews and non-Jews. All hell broke loose in most places he went. But that was not because his mission included a new religion and communities discon-nected from Jews and Judaism.

Paul was persuaded that the kingdom of God had broken in and the time had come for Jews and Gentiles to unite to worship the one true God under the messianic headship of Jesus. It was a dangerous, radical, divisive, and weird mission.

Some would say, both then and now, that Paul's conviction about Jesus was a misstep that destined his entire enterprise to go awry. Of course, Paul's judgment about Jesus, as well as our own, is a matter of personal belief. But regardless of one's viewpoint, it behooves everyone to get the story right about this one-of-a-kind global influencer. And Paul's mission is a big part of his story—and the story of the world.

Simply stated, here is the game-changing idea regarding Paul: His mission was not to start a new religion or plant churches as we think of them today. His mission was to call Gentiles to abandon their idols and give singular loyalty and worship to the Jewish God because of the death and resurrection of Jesus. This mission, Paul believed, would result in diverse assemblies of Jews and Gentiles orienting their devo-tion to Jesus according to the principles of the Torah and in accord with the vision of the prophets.

GAME-CHANGING ACTION

Contrary to the intent of Paul's mission, Christianity and Judaism developed into two distinct religions. And along with this parting of the ways has come theological and, at times, tangible hostility between Christians and Jews.

There are many reasons why most Jews disagree with Paul's perspec-tive about Jesus. Paul was persuaded that Jesus was the Messiah. Most Jews, then and now, have not been convinced. However, Jews do not have to agree with Paul about Jesus to begin seeing his mission in a new, more positive light. Paul is best understood as an emissary of Judaism. It would be tough to argue that there has ever been a Jewish person more impactful in extending the principles of Judaism to the world than Paul—despite how his later interpreters severed the apostle from his native religion.

But in recent times, there are Jews who are seeking to reposition Paul within the space that they argue he never left. A growing movement of Jewish scholars are reframing Paul within Judaism. And this movement, in addition to presenting a more historically accurate picture of Paul, has the potential to shift how the Jewish community categorizes Paul. Rather than seeing him as a traitor, Jews can once again see him as one of their own—who, despite getting some things wrong, got a lot right regarding his endeavors to bring the God of Israel to the world. Michael Wyschogrod expressed such sentiments in his book *Abraham's Promise*:

> This is what we can learn from Paul. We can learn from him that Israel has a responsibility to enable gentiles to obey its God and live in covenant with him. For Paul, this possibility centers on and is inconceivable without Christ. But it must also become a possibility for Judaism within its own framework. . . . The non-election of the gentiles cannot be as deep and permanent as Judaism has often assumed. This is the truth of Paul.[43]

Because of the way Paul has been framed, Jews have generally not seen him as a figure who can offer them the truth on any level. Wyschogrod saw different possibilities, and many Jews are beginning to as well. This is not an easy step for the Jewish community, but it will hopefully continue to progress.

For Christians, seeing Paul as a Jewish emissary who sought to bring Judaism's Redeemer to Gentiles can help dampen the sense that Jews and Judaism are seen as "others." For Christians, a new way of thinking about Paul could go like this: Paul loved Jesus, and that love was something he expressed as a representative of Judaism. Paul didn't reject his own Jewish people or Judaism. And he never taught Gentiles that they replaced Jews as God's people. Rather, because of Jesus, Paul's mission was centered on offering Gentiles a way to be transformed from sinners into holy people who could join the Jewish people in the end-times family of God.

So, let's be honest. Jews and Christians have some significant differences. And those differences should be respected. But those differences should not be based on assumptions about Paul that frame him as against, over, or outside of Judaism. Paul's mission was weird. And radical. And controversial. But it did not include starting a new religion called Christianity and planting churches that were disconnected from Jews and Judaism.

Numerous contemporary factors continue justifying clear borders between Christians and Jews. However, making Paul weird again offers significant possibilities for the two groups to move closer together. A Jewish Paul may sound and feel strange. But it is a Paul who can once again promote kinship and shalom across those borders.

CHAPTER 4

Paul's Weird Message

A new perspective on an old message

3:00 A.M.

Sleepless nights.

I'm confident you and I would agree that, usually, they are *not* a good thing.

Maybe "good" is not the right word. Perhaps a better way of putting it is that sleepless nights are not a comfortable thing. Sometimes sleepless nights, while uncomfortable, can bring forth gold.

Some of the most important decisions I have ever made came from insights on sleepless nights. Because of this pattern, a few years ago, I wrote a memoir called *3:00 AM*, in which I shared some of my most significant "3:00 a.m. moments" and the light that came in those dark hours. I wrote this memoir for my kids. It was also cathartic for me. In *3:00 AM*, I shared honestly about wrestling with myself and God. I wrote about deconstruction and reconstruction, doubt and faith, death and resurrection, getting my butt kicked, and getting up off the mat.

Something about the middle of the night brings out the raw, real stuff. If it wakes you up and even gets you out of bed, it matters.

WAKING THE WEIRD APOSTLE

I wonder what were the things that gave Paul sleepless nights. We know he had them. He wrote to the community at Corinth that he had "many sleepless nights" (2 Cor 11:27).

What was it that woke the Weird Apostle at 3:00 a.m.? Paul said, "There is the daily pressure on me of my anxiety for all the churches" (2 Cor 11:28). Based on his flow of thought, it appears Paul's sleepless nights were linked to his concern for the fledgling communities he helped to form. But that still doesn't tell us much.

What was Paul anxious about? Does he offer any clues in his letters? I think he does.

There *was* an issue Paul was repeatedly defensive, angry, and anxious about in his letters. Paul started swinging in his letters (and lost sleep at night) because he believed his Gentiles were being influenced to divert from or, in some cases, altogether abandon the message he announced.

To Paul, as weird as it may have sounded to his contemporaries, his message was the one, true, and only gospel that could transform non-Jews from sinners to saints. Paul frequently referred to his message to non-Jews as *euangelion*—a Greek word that translates as "gospel" or "good news."

Not everyone assessed Paul's message as good. We only have a record of Paul's side of the story, but his letters signal more than a few negative responses to his message. Kickback came from groups Paul viewed as competitors. Other backlash came from local Jewish and Gentile community members who felt Paul's message did not accord with local norms and protocols.

Paul tossed, turned, and I imagine occasionally rose at 3:00 a.m. for a clear and consistent reason: He feared some of his Gentiles would abandon his gospel in response to the pressure they faced.

DOUBTING WHAT WE'RE SURE OF

We know what Paul's message is. And we know what Paul's gospel is. Jesus lived, died, and rose from the dead so that all who believe in him can be forgiven, avoid hell, and have a way to heaven. That's certainly an important message. And it's familiar.

I tend to think that in my theoretical meeting with Paul, he would call for another round when this topic comes up. I can see him leaning over and saying, "Ryan, the message typically referred to as 'the gospel' today is far from mine. A new perspective is needed."

Yes, we need a new perspective on Paul's weird gospel message. But change can be hard. And it is especially difficult to question things we are sure of. And for many, one of those sure things is the gospel.

But what if questioning our view of the gospel produces a new outlook that gives us a greater appreciation for that message?

THE NEW PERSPECTIVE ON PAUL

For most of the past two thousand years, it was an unquestioned assumption that Paul's gospel stood in sharp contrast to the Judaism of his day. But in the 1960s, a new movement led some scholars to question this framework. This movement was called "the New Perspective on Paul."[44] As the '60s produced upheaval in many cultural institutions, this small but powerful movement disrupted the world of New Testament studies and research. Bible scholars such as E. P. Sanders and Krister Stendahl began challenging standard Christian assumptions about the Judaism of Paul's time. A central assumption these New Perspective scholars questioned was the prevailing Christian characterization of Judaism as a religion filled with self-righteousness and legalism. New Perspective scholars saw little evidence for these ideas in ancient Jewish sources.

In his watershed book *Paul and Palestinian Judaism*, Sanders, a Duke University professor, presented the results of his exhaustive research of Jewish texts ranging from 200 BCE to 200 CE. Sanders saw a pattern of thinking he labeled "covenantal nomism."

In contrast to traditional Christian caricatures of the Judaism of Paul's time, Sanders's analysis revealed that Jews in the time of Jesus and Paul did not observe the Torah with the mindset that their devotion earned their salvation or a righteous standing with God. Instead, Sanders concluded that Jews kept the Torah to confirm and express their covenant relationship with the God of Israel. Sanders wrote:

> In discussing disobedience and obedience, punishment and reward, [the Rabbis] were not dealing with how man is saved, but with how man should act and how God will act within the framework of the covenant. . . . They did not think that they earned their place in the covenant by the number of mitzvoth [commandments] fulfilled. Nor did they believe that the transgression of more commandments than were fulfilled would damn them.[45]

Sanders's research convincingly demonstrated several things that have a huge impact on how we understand Paul's gospel message:

1. Jews, in Paul's day and in ours, believe their covenant relationship with God was established by his grace and mercy, not by their merit.
2. Jews, in Paul's day and in ours, believe good deeds, obedience, and works are the fitting actions of people *already* in a covenant relationship with God.
3. Some Jews (not unlike some Christians) can be legalistic. But legalism and "salvation by works" do not characterize the Judaism of Paul's day or ours.

Jewish scholar Pamela Eisenbaum's comments on the impact of the New Perspective are enlightening:

New-perspective scholars are committed to undoing the misconstrual of Judaism that has accompanied the traditional understanding of Paul. . . . In contrast to Christianity conceived by Christians as a religion of spirit, grace, and love, Judaism has been construed as a religion of law, in which salvation must be earned and which produces adherents who legalistically calculate their accumulation of merit, brashly boast of their accomplishments, lack any notion of grace, and are devoid of spiritual sentiment in their religious practice. This characterization of Judaism is a gross distortion, both in general terms and in the first century. Thus, any interpretation of Paul that promulgates or relies on such a view to draw conclusions about what Paul said should be repudiated. Instead, Paul's letters must be contextualized within a historically plausible reconstruction of first-century Judaism.[46]

Most interpretations of Paul have relied on the "old perspective" of Judaism as a graceless religion. Perhaps in this sense, for Christians at least, Judaism should also be made weird again to reflect a more historically accurate representation of the Jewish faith.

Okay, here's what we can pull together from the above points. If earning salvation through good works was not a Jewish viewpoint in Paul's day, then it could not have been a viewpoint that Paul's gospel countered. Thus, if Paul's message did not aim to replace salvation by works or legalism, what purpose did it serve?

We'll tackle that question. But first, I want to share another frame from my personal story.

THE NEW PERSPECTIVE AND MY OWN EXPERIENCE

I am Jewish. But at one point in my life, most of what I knew about Judaism came from Christian sources. From those sources, I also concluded Judaism teaches that one merits their standing with God through an accumulation of good works.

But something big happened that changed my perspective. I started interacting with Jewish sources firsthand. When I began direct contact with the Talmud, the Midrash, and the Shulchan Aruch, I saw that Judaism differed from what I had learned. And when I began practicing Judaism and participating in a local synagogue, it became even more apparent to me that Judaism is a way of life that cultivates a deep dependence upon the grace and mercy of God.

One of many examples of the emphasis on the mercy of God in Judaism is found in the Tachanun prayer. Tachanun is recited from the Jewish Prayer book, the siddur, in synagogues on Mondays and Thursdays. Here is an excerpt:

He, the Merciful One, is forgiving of iniquity and does not destroy, frequently withdrawing his anger, not arousing his entire rage. You, Hashem—withhold not your mercy from us; may your kindness and your truth always protect us.[47]

If these lines ring familiar to you, that's because they are pulled directly from Psalms 78 and 40. Most importantly, Tachanun does not sound like the prayer of a self-righteous petitioner who believes they can do enough deeds to win favor with God. Instead, it is a prayer that reflects a heartfelt plea for God's compassion.

The humility and mercy expressed in the Tachanun prayer is not an exception in Judaism. It is normal. Prayers and expressions such as these have characterized Judaism through the ages.

Paul's gospel did not serve to counter Jewish legalism. That's because legalism does not characterize Judaism—in Paul's day or in ours. So, if Paul's weird, good-news message had nothing to do with convincing Jews and Gentiles that trying to earn their salvation through enough good deeds was futile, then what problem did his gospel aim to solve?

As we'll find out, Paul's message had everything to do with announcing to Gentiles how the death and resurrection of Jesus could make them members in equal standing within the family of God.

LET'S PUMP THE BREAKS

I hear you saying, "Whoa, are you suggesting Paul's gospel was exclusively directed to Gentiles? I'm not sure about that. He seemed to say a lot about Jews and Jewish stuff. How could his gospel only be for Gentiles?"

You are correct that Paul talked a lot about Jews and Jewish stuff. It's all over his letters. As a Jewish teacher spreading a Jewish message, it makes all the sense in the world that Paul's letters were saturated with a Jewish flavor. And, yes, Paul's gospel was "to the Jew first" (Rom 1:16).

But for Paul, Jews were already members of the family of God. They are "elect" and "beloved," and their "gifts and callings are irrevocable" (Rom 11:28–29). That is powerful and clear language from Paul, which affirms that his Jewish brothers have a secure relationship with God. And it's as if Paul wants the depth and the commitment of this relationship to be beyond a shadow of a doubt when he says of his fellow Jews that "to them belongs the adoption as sons, the glory, the covenants, and the giving of the Torah" (Rom 9:3–4). Paul was emphatic about the unchanging nature of God's commitment and bond with the Jewish people.

Now, does that mean Paul thought his Jewish brothers could ignore Jesus? Absolutely not.

Without a doubt, Paul wanted his fellow Jews to embrace Jesus as the king of Israel and the Messianic Redeemer (Rom 10:1–4). And Paul was brokenhearted over the lackluster receptivity among his Jewish brethren concerning Jesus (Rom 9:3–4).

But Paul's mission and message had a particular focus. His gospel, as apostle to the Gentiles, was to announce the ground-shaking implications of Jesus's death and resurrection for Gentiles. And at the core of his message was the weird, strange, radical idea that the God of the Jews is the God of all people. Thus:

- The Jewish God was not bound by geography—which was different from the limited spatial reach of the Greco-Roman gods.
- The Jewish God did not discriminate between peoples—which differed from the gods, who prioritized the people in their locales.
- And the Jewish God was only one God—which differed from the polytheistic, god-congested culture Paul's Gentiles were part of.

This was a weird, bold message for a Jewish teacher to direct to Gentiles.

BUT WAIT, THERE'S MORE

When my friend and colleague Rabbi Jason Sobel gets fired up during a flow, he is known to say, "But wait, there's more!"

And there's always more with Paul.

The "more" of Paul's weird gospel is that because of the non-Jews' trusting allegiance to Jesus, and the transformative power of God's Spirit, which now defined their new nature, non-Jews could be fully integrated and justified as members of God's family. This, for Paul, was what justification by faith was all about. This was his gospel.

But this was a weird message.

If you were a Gentile hearing Paul's good news directly from him or through one of his letters, you likely would have questions—lots of them. Think of yourself as a pagan in Corinth or a Gentile god-fearer in Athens. What would you have wanted Paul to clarify? Sure, we have plenty of modern questions for the Weird Apostle. But if we were in their shoes, in Paul's day, what would we be asking?

FAIR QUESTIONS FOR PAUL

Based on his letters and what we know regarding Paul's historical context, these could have been some of the questions he would have received, and how he might have responded.

First-century Gentile question: Okay, Paul, I've bought into your message. I believe Jesus rose from the dead. And now I am following the Jewish God, like the Jews. So, doesn't that mean I should become a Jew?

Paul's possible answer: No, that's the whole point! By trusting in Jesus's redeeming work, God's spirit has come to live inside you. You now have a new nature—the old has gone and the new has come. You have been "righteous-ed" *as a Gentile* through Jesus.

And here's why that's important. God is not just the God of the Jews. He is the God of the Gentiles as well. So, you need to remain as a Gentile. Doing so represents that one God is God of the whole earth and all people.

The Jewish prophets envisioned a day would come when all the world would recognize that the God of the Jews is the God of all people. Jesus's justifying work produces shalom, unity, and equality between Jews and Gentiles. It does not make either group into the other.

To be clear, you do not have to become a Jew to follow the God of the Jews. In fact, you *must* remain a member of the nations to demonstrate that God is the God of every tongue, nation, and people. If non-Jews have to convert and become Jews, that implies that God is *only* the God of the Jews, right? Well, I'm here to give you some good news. The God of Israel is much bigger than that. He is Lord of the entire earth. Attach yourself to Jesus, and you are good to go!

First-century Gentile question: I want to be sure I understand your message, Paul, because what I think I understand is not only weird, but frightening. Are you saying that if I follow the Jewish God, then I can't follow my native gods? Because if that's what you are saying, I will face a lot of pushback from my family and friends. Why in the world would I do this?

Paul's possible answer: You are correct. For us, there is only one God, the Father, who is in heaven. And we have one master, Jesus, our Messiah.

I understand that not following the gods you have known your whole life will create significant problems. But I want to encourage you with this. Following Jesus will be of far greater benefit to you.

I understand what it's like to set aside an easier life. Things could have been much easier for me too. I have all kinds of credentials that would have given me a good life among my people. But in many ways, I've set those credentials aside because I have accepted a calling from God that has created a deep tension between me and most of my Jewish brothers and sisters.

But let me assure you, it's worth it. By staying connected to this Jewish message, as an in-Christ Gentile, you will experience benefits in this life, and in the future, that far outweigh the difficulties we face now. You now have a relationship with the one true God. You are now connected to his family. You can now call God your Father. You are now reconciled to him. You have been cleansed and washed. You are no longer associated with the sinfulness of idolatry.

All this is amazing. And you now have a sense of assurance that when Jesus returns, which will happen soon, you will be gathered to God and fully prepared to enjoy life in the next world. And that world is full of joy, peace, and oneness with God.

First-century Gentile question: I believe what you are saying about the Jewish God and Jesus. But I was hoping you could sort this out for me a bit.

I understand that I can't worship my gods and I can only worship the Jewish God. And I also know you are saying I can't become a Jew either—which I see as a problem because that's what people in my community will expect me to do if I want to do all this Jewish stuff. I've heard of some folks in these parts who decided to become Jews. It's frowned upon, but it's acceptable. But again, you are saying conversion is not an option.

So . . . you want us to follow the Jewish God and live a Jewish-*ish* lifestyle, but we can't become Jews—then where does that leave me?

Am I a "Jewish Gentile"? I don't mean to be funny. But I don't understand where I stand in all this. What in the world am I, Paul?

Paul's possible answer: Yes, you are in a difficult place. Making all this even worse is that other Jewish groups say you need to go through a conversion process to become legally Jewish if you want to be members of equal standing among God's people. And on the other side, you have Gentile groups trying to pull you back to pagan forms of worship—which, in their minds, is where you belong.

So please know that while I am not in your shoes, I sympathize with your tenuous position.

You asked me what you are. I'll try to be as clear as possible: You are an adopted, holy member of Abraham's family—the family of God.

God made covenants with my Jewish people and continues to see them as beloved despite their widespread rejection of Jesus. But in this new age, which was launched by Jesus's death and resurrection, you are now citizens in God's kingdom and members of God's family because of your new nature and standing in Jesus.

So, who are you? You are holy ones and adopted children of God. I like to think that what God did through Jesus, and is currently doing through the Holy Spirit, is a mystery revealed.

And what he is doing among you Gentiles, here and everywhere, indicates that what the Jewish prophets expected at the end of time is unfolding before our eyes. And be encouraged—soon, Jesus will return, and all your suffering and challenges will be worth it. I promise.

SEO, KEYWORDS, AND PAUL

Before we wrap up our discussion of Paul's weird message, I want to underscore the importance of a few keywords Paul used in the previous imagined exchange.

Clearly, I have a significant interest and investment in Jewish-Christian relations and education. However, my professional, personal, and research interests take me into additional realms. I love exploring game-changing ideas in health, leadership, self-improvement, and relationships.[48] And I dabble in marketing as well.[49]

In marketing, I enjoy learning about the power of search engine optimization (SEO) in growing the popularity of websites and other online assets. SEO refers to a strategy and process to make a web page appear higher on a list when people search for topics. One of the keys to having good SEO and ranking high in online searches is ensuring your web content contains keywords that people include when searching for specific topics.

Paul also had some keywords that appeared frequently in his letters. He regularly utilized these terms in innovative ways to explain his weird message.

Three primary keywords are paramount as we consider Paul's groundbreaking message:

1. Adoption. For Paul, adoption as sons and daughters was something God initiated for the Jewish people long ago (see Exod 4:22). And he expressed that their adoption and sonship were immovable, whether they had *pistis* in Christ or not. Speaking of his Jewish brothers and sisters, he said: "They are Israelites, and to them belong the *adoption*, the glory, the covenants, the giving of the law, the worship, and the promises" (Rom 9:4).

Central to Paul's message was that because of Christ, non-Jews could also be "adopted" into God's family while remaining as non-Jews:

> But when the fullness of time had come, God sent forth his Son, born of woman, born under the law, to redeem those who were under the law, so that we might receive adoption as sons. And because you are sons, God has sent the Spirit of his Son into our hearts, crying, "Abba! Father!" So you are no longer a slave, but a son, and if a son, then an heir through God. (Gal 3:4–7)

Adoption (*huiothesia* in Greek) was central to Paul's Jewish message of redemption for Gentiles. However, it was not unique to Judaism. Adoption frameworks and processes were present in the Roman culture of Paul's audience. Paula Fredriksen notes:

> Paul's ideas on Gentile adoption in (and into) Christ reveal his thought at one and the same time at its most Roman, at its most traditionally Jewish, and at its most ancient. Roman legal culture had long availed itself of this form of fictive kinship— sons not begotten but made—as a way to settle and to stabilize the next generation of "family" both for issues of property/inheritance and for issues of ancestry/continuation of patrilineal cult. The new son was thereafter responsible to and for his "new" paternal ancestors and to and for . . . his new father and family.[50]

According to Fredriksen, when Paul used adoption language in his letters, his Greco-Roman recipients had an existing framework for the dynamics he described. This would increase their ability to internalize their new status as fully adopted sons and daughters within the family of Israel's God. Paul uses such language in Romans 8:15–17 when he says:

> For you did not receive the spirit of slavery to fall back into fear, but you have received the Spirit of adoption as sons, by whom we cry, "Abba! Father!" The Spirit himself bears witness with our spirit that we are children of God, and if children, then heirs—heirs of God and fellow heirs with Christ, provided we suffer with him in order that we may also be glorified with him.

Paul's letters consistently seek to persuade his non-Jewish audience to understand themselves as adopted brothers and sisters alongside the Jewish people. Because Paul's non-Jews were now in-Christ, they could call the Jewish God "Abba! Father!" Fredriksen and Matthew Thiessen aptly describe what Jews and Gentiles in Christ now share as a result of Paul's gospel message:

> Gentile adoption was accomplished by Christ's spirit or through holy spirit, that these non-Jews, as adopted "brothers" (*adelphoi*), share a connection to Abraham (Gal 3:16, 26; Rom 4:16–17). They, like (the then still uncircumcised) Abraham, "trust" (*pisteuo*) in God's promises that they, too, will be blessed (Gal 3:8; Gen 12:3). They thereby through their own trust (*pistis*) mimetically share in Abraham's "righteousness" (Rom 4:9; Gen 15:6). They too, like Jews, can now address the Jewish god as "Father" (Rom 8:15; Gal 4:6).[51]

2. Mystery. A second keyword Paul uses to describe his message is *mysterion* (Greek for "mystery"). This term appears in multiple Pauline letters. However, "mystery" is used with particular richness in Ephesians (emphasis my own):

When you read this, you can perceive my insight into the **mystery** of Christ, which was not made known to the sons of men in other generations as it has now been revealed to his holy apostles and prophets by the Spirit. This **mystery** is that the Gentiles are fellow heirs, members of the same body, and partakers of the promise in Christ Jesus through the gospel. Of this gospel I was made a minister according to the gift of God's grace, which was given me by the working of his power. To me, though I am the very least of all the saints, this grace was given, to preach to the Gentiles the unsearchable riches of Christ, and to bring to light for everyone what is the plan of the **mystery** hidden for ages in God. (Eph 3:4–9)

This text is a rare example of Paul using a graphic term *and* telling us exactly how he uses it. Still, among commentators, there is a lack of clarity regarding how Paul uses *mysterion* in this text.

What is the "mystery" Paul refers to? Many think it was that Gentiles could experience redemption. But that was not really a mystery. Plenty of biblical texts include a vision of redemption that includes Gentiles. One such text is Zechariah 8:21–23:

Thus says the Lord of hosts: Peoples shall yet come, even the inhabitants of many cities. The inhabitants of one city shall go to another, saying, "Let us go at once to entreat the favor of the Lord and to seek the Lord of hosts; I myself am going." Many peoples and strong nations shall come to seek the Lord of hosts in Jerusalem and to entreat the favor of the Lord. Thus says the Lord of hosts: In those days ten men from the nations of every tongue shall take hold of the robe of a Jew, saying, "Let us go with you, for we have heard that God is with you."

Texts like Zechariah 8 led at least some Jews in Paul's day to believe non-Jews would eventually be redeemed and included in the world to come. But Jewish sources were hazy and reluctant to project specifically *how* idolatrous, sinful (from a Jewish outlook) non-Jews would gain such a standing.

In other words, how would pagans join God's family in the end? Well, it was a mystery. But Paul was convinced the mystery of "how" had been revealed.

Christian scholar Lionel Windsor provides keen insight into the nature of the mystery described in Ephesians 3:

> What is the "new" element of the revelation when it comes to the gentiles? It cannot be referring simply to the fact that gentiles are now blessed through Israel, nor that gentiles are now included in temple worship. Those things were already anticipated in the Scriptures, and so cannot be described as a "mystery." Furthermore, Paul cannot be simply claiming that gentile inclusion is now understood or known to a greater extent than it was before the advent of Christ. The language of "revelation" and "hiddenness" implies that something genuinely new has been revealed, something that was not previously known at all. . . . The mystery that has been revealed involves the equality of status between Jews and Gentiles in Christ. . . . This full equality of status was not clear in the prophetic Scriptures and other Jewish writings, which often portrayed the nations as politically subservient to Israel at the eschaton.[52]

According to Windsor, Paul's mystery revealed that in-Christ Gentiles now had "full equality of status." This was a radical, weird component of Paul's gospel. And lots of Paul's Jewish brethren were not buying it.

It's one thing to say Gentiles would be transformed, redeemed, and adopted into the family of God. That was no mystery.

It's another thing—and a very weird, uncomfortable thing—for a

Jew to proclaim Gentiles were now equals within that family because of Christ.

That was not expected. It was a mystery that Paul's gospel message now revealed.

3. Saints/holy ones. Another Pauline keyword is "saints," or some prefer "holy ones." Paul's Greek term for "saints" in his letters is *hagios*. The parallel Hebrew word is *kedoshim*.

In Paul's day, when Jews spoke of saints or holy ones in either Greek or Hebrew, they consistently referred to other Jews. Non-Jews most definitely were *not* categorized as holy ones or saints.

Thus, for Paul to categorize in-Christ Gentiles as saints would be a gear-grinder to Jewish ears. This practice was representative of Paul's larger enterprise of redrawing the boundary lines of humanity. It was a weird, new, and radical idea that non-Jews could now also be saints/holy ones/*hagios*/*kedoshim* alongside the Jewish people.

In Paul's mind, before Jesus, to be a Gentile was to be a pagan, and to be a pagan was to be a Gentile. As Thiessen and Fredriksen note, "There were no religion-neutral ethnicities in Paul's lifetime—one of the reasons that his biblical term for non-Jews, *ta ethne*, is better translated with the religion-specific term 'pagans' than with the seemingly religion-neutral 'gentiles.'"[53]

A "holy" pagan or "saintly" Gentile was an impossibility from a Jewish standpoint. But border lines were changing according to Paul's weird, good-news message.

According to Paul and because of the apocalyptic and messianic ramifications of Jesus's death and resurrection, pagan Gentiles who were categorically unholy (or "sinners," as Paul said in Gal 2:15) can be declared holy ones alongside Jews.

For a Jew to categorize non-Jews as "holy" and "equal" may sound normal to us. But to first-century ears, this was a weird, shocking designation.

LET'S SUM THIS UP

When I played baseball, several of my coaches emphasized this acronym: KISS, or **k**eep **i**t **s**imple, **s**tupid! In other words, don't over-analyze or overthink your mechanics, approach, and all things mental when it comes to playing the game.

Sure, they would say, you need to have a good approach and be an intelligent player. But there comes a time when you must be an athlete and go out there, play the game, and have fun.

Keeping it simple can help athletes. It's also useful when studying Paul.

But as you probably know, keeping it simple with Paul is . . . not so simple. But it doesn't mean we shouldn't try. By making Paul weird, we do simplify him and make him more understandable, compelling, and impactful.

So, for the sake of simplicity, let's sum up Paul's weird gospel message. And I'll practice KISS by keeping it to simple bullet points regarding what it's not and what it is.

PAUL'S GOSPEL MESSAGE: WHAT IT'S NOT

1. It was not a message designed to counter Judaism or the Torah.
2. It was not a message designed to provide an alternative to legalism—which is a way of understanding salvation or redemption via the accumulation of works or deeds.
3. It was *not* a message that targeted Jews. Yes, Paul wanted his Jewish brothers and sisters to embrace Jesus. But Paul wanted Jews to embrace Jesus within their already existing, irrevocable covenant relationship with God. Specifically as part of his mission, Paul articulated his gospel as a message *to Gentiles* as a path to become justified, adopted members of equal standing within God's family.

PAUL'S GOSPEL MESSAGE: WHAT IT IS

1. It was a message for non-Jews—who, from a Jewish standpoint, were sinners, pagans, and idolaters.

2. It was a message calling Gentiles to turn from the gods and give singular allegiance to the God of the Jews.

3. It was a message that revolved around Jesus's death and resurrection—which, if Gentiles would trust it, could supernaturally transform them from being governed by the flesh to being ruled by the Spirit of God. This new nature enabled holy, Torah-informed living commensurate with life within Abraham's family and alongside the Jewish people.

A 3:00 A.M. GAME CHANGER

What is Paul's gospel? There is perhaps no more significant question for Christians. And for Jews, how Christians answer is a significant factor in how a relationship between the parties can proceed.

It's time for an updated answer to this question.

Paul's gospel was what he lived and died for. Protecting it woke him up at 3:00 a.m. and gave him plenty of sleepless nights. It also made him one of the most influential people in history.

But Paul's gospel message has been distorted for a very long time. It has been made too familiar and forced to solve problems that were foreign to Paul.

Paul's gospel message did not provide a new (Christian) grace-based way of salvation through Jesus that toppled a (Jewish) legalistic, works-based path of salvation. Jews were not legalists and they did not believe works saved people. Both in Paul's day and in ours, Jews believe that a relationship with God is based on trusting him, loving him, and obeying his commandments.

Paul's gospel was a weird, innovative message that focused on the redemption of non-Jews. His message offered a way for Gentiles to join the family of God, alongside Jews, and obtain a holy, equal, justified status through their identification with Jesus's death and resurrection and their new Spirit-inhabited nature.

This breakthrough message radically changed the game in Paul's day. And a return to this understanding of Paul's gospel can change the game in ours.

GAME-CHANGING ACTION

As I get older, I realize most people tend to lean in one of two directions regarding relationships. Most of us have a pattern of being peacemakers or peace-breakers.

Sure, folks who are typically good at establishing peace can sometimes be disruptive. On the other side, folks who aren't afraid to stir things up can also effectively bring parties together.

Most of us tend to lean one way or the other. I tend to be a peacemaker. I've certainly found myself in more than a few frays, but for the most part, I like to smooth things over rather than stir the pot.

Something I've learned through my years of experience in Jewish-Christian relations is the importance of *not* smoothing things over and minimizing differences. Regardless of Jesus's and Paul's intent, Judaism and Christianity developed very differently. And the differences between the two faiths are massive. Ignoring or minimizing those differences does not always help improve relations between them. But returning Paul's message to its first-century context can create a game-changing interconnection that has been missing for two thousand years.

What if a Christian understanding of Paul viewed his gospel as the means by which non-Jewish followers of Jesus can walk as equal, adopted, and holy members within the family of God? This mysterious dynamic, by Paul's account, made possible by the atoning death of Jesus, does not require denigrating Judaism. Christians do not need to characterize Judaism as bankrupt or legalistic to make Jesus and the gospel message look good.

And what if more Jews understood Paul's gospel as, at the very least, an attempt to bring non-Jews into a transformative relationship with the God of Israel? Jews disagree that Jesus is the Messiah. And they have significant differences with various tenets of Christianity. But it would be a game changer for more Jews to see Paul as the initial catalyst for a movement dedicated to creating a space for non-Jews to sit at Abraham's family table.

Traditional ways of understanding Paul's gospel message have created problems and divisions that would have been foreign to the apostle. Returning his message to its unfamiliar, weird setting can help build bridges between the people who mattered most to the Weird Apostle—namely, his Jewish brethren and his non-Jewish Christ-followers. Such a renewed hope, I believe, would drive the apostle to rise out of bed with energy and excitement—even after a sleepless night.

CHAPTER 5

Paul's Weird View of Time

Paul's fast-moving watch deeply impacted his letters

TO MEASURE A MOMENT

To measure a moment, go by weight and not by size
The big ones may look great, but they can be hollow inside
If you are so lucky to find a moment, don't hold on
'Cause you won't know the weight of a moment
Until it's gone

The thing about a moment is it's a fleeting point in time
The river keeps on moving, unrelenting in its tide
So if you hate what's happened to a moment, don't hold on
Because it only takes a moment for this moment
To be gone
A moment's a length, but it's immeasurable by time
It's not the ticking of a clock, it's not seconds passing by
You see, there's moments between moments when time doesn't move at all
It's the time it takes to fall in love and it's the love that will break your fall
—"To Measure a Moment," Highbeams

That song saved me once upon a time. Of course, it's not actually a song that saves us. But a song can awaken hope and inspiration during difficult times.

Certain songs just resonate deep down and catalyze us to take the heavy, daring steps from night's thick darkness to the hopeful outskirts of dawn.

"To Measure a Moment" by Highbeams did that for me during one of the most difficult periods of my life. I am grateful to Adam, Ian, and Stephen for their moving song that reminded me of the simple and healing truth that we don't have to hold on to bad, weighty moments. The river keeps on moving, unrelenting in its tide. Bad moments or seasons can change quickly into a positive flow if we allow time and ourselves to keep moving forward. As the song goes, "It's the time it takes to fall in love and it's the love that will break your fall."

PAUL'S FAST-MOVING METER

As Highbeams sings, you won't know the weight of a moment . . . until it's gone. But one thing we can count on is this: Time keeps moving unrelentingly.

How fast we perceive the river to be moving is a significant factor in how we see the world and, thus, how we live. If we are convinced we have plenty of time, it tends to reduce our sense of immanency and extend our outlook and planning. If we are confident time is short, it speeds up our movement and reduces the length of our vision.

Paul had a very short-term view of time. The Weird Apostle was persuaded that Jesus's return and the end of the world were at hand. And the few moments left on *his* watch deeply influenced how he advised his followers and crafted his letters.

PAUL'S SURPRISE

Paul would be shocked to learn his letters continue to be immeasurably valued two thousand years after he composed them.

But his surprise would not be over the value part. Paul was in a unique category of people who testified to being personally commissioned by Jesus. He knew his letters and position carried weight among early Jesus-followers. That would be no bombshell for him.

Paul's astonishment would have everything to do with *time*. It would bewilder him that Jesus had not returned two thousand years later. In multiple letters, Paul wrote that he expected Jesus to return within his lifetime:

> For this we declare to you by a word from the Lord, that we who are alive, who are left until the coming of the Lord, will not precede those who have fallen asleep. For the Lord himself will descend from heaven with a cry of command, with the voice of an archangel, and with the sound of the trumpet of God. And the dead in Christ will rise first. **Then we who are alive, who are left, will be caught up together with them in the clouds to meet the Lord in the air,** and so we will always be with the Lord. Therefore encourage one another with these words. (1 Thess 4:15–18)

This is what I mean, brothers: **the appointed time has grown very short.** From now on, let those who have wives live as though they had none, and those who mourn as though they were not mourning, and those who rejoice as though they were not rejoicing, and those who buy as though they had no goods, and those who deal with the world as though they had no dealings with it. **For the present form of this world is passing away.** (1 Cor 7:29–31)

Now these things happened to them as an example, but they were written down for our instruction, on whom **the end of the ages has come.** (1 Cor 10:11)

Paul thought heaven and earth would soon change drastically upon Jesus's return. Thus, he wrote his letters to address circumstances that would, in his mind, soon expire.

Paul had a weird, short-term view of time.

PAUL ACROSS TIME

Christians classify Paul's letters as timeless and inspired. His words are holy Scripture. But even for those who do not embrace Paul's letters as God's word yet share an interest in him, they frequently share an inattentiveness regarding how fast he believed time was progressing toward Jesus's return and the end of the age. Paul was not playing the long game.

It is a short path to entanglement if Paul's readers and interpreters do not consider his fast-moving watch. To stay free of such knots, it is important to remember some key ideas about how Paul operated in relation to time.

But first, let's discuss a question that frequently arises when considering Paul's clock: Was Paul incorrect in his expectation about when Jesus would return?

WAS PAUL'S CLOCK WRONG?

For those who embrace Paul's letters as Scripture, it can be unsettling to consider that the apostle may have been wrong about the timing of Jesus's return. And this can lead to pressed interpretations that aim to clear the apostle of unfulfilled, time-sensitive expectations.

An example of this kind of reading is found in the popular *ESV Study Bible's* commentary on 1 Thessalonians 4:15: "For this we declare to you by a word from the Lord, that **we who are alive**, who are left until the coming of the Lord, will not precede those who have fallen asleep."

This statement indicates Paul's confidence that he would live to see Jesus's return. But the *ESV Study Bible* has a different take: "**We who are alive** does not imply that Paul was convinced that he would be alive at the second coming, but rather that all Christians should be prepared for Christ to return during their lifetime."[54]

My take is that the *ESV Study Bible* is straining to get Paul off the hook for personally expecting to witness Jesus's return—which did not, in fact, happen. But is Paul really on the hook for expecting to see Jesus's return? Does his statement in 1 Thessalonians 4:15 prove he was wrong or misguided? This is not so black and white.

Paul's forecast for a soon-arriving global redemption connected him to a long chain of apocalyptic, Jewish, prophetic characters who also believed the age of redemption would begin in their lifetime (or close to it).

The Jewish prophet Haggai expressed grand, redemptive expectations for the post-exilic (after the Babylonian captivity) Jerusalem Temple. Haggai's prophetic utterance pointed to salvific realities that he expected to occur during the Second Temple period, which ended almost two thousand years ago:

For thus says the Lord of hosts: Yet once more, in a little while,
I will shake the heavens and the earth and the sea and the dry

land. And I will shake all nations, so that the treasures of all nations shall come in, and I will fill this house with glory, says the Lord of hosts. The silver is mine, and the gold is mine, declares the Lord of hosts. The latter glory of this house shall be greater than the former, says the Lord of hosts. And in this place I will give peace, declares the Lord of hosts. (Haggai 2:6–9)

According to this text, Haggai expected immense glory and peace in the Second Temple—which would eclipse what was enjoyed in Solomon's Temple ("the former" house). But, in fact, no such realities were enjoyed by Jews during the Second Temple period.

Were Haggai's prophetic expectations wrong?

Jesus also communicated redemptive expectations that were not fulfilled in accordance with the timeline he communicated:

Then will appear in heaven the sign of the Son of Man, and then all the tribes of the earth will mourn, and they will see the Son of Man coming on the clouds of heaven with power and great glory. . . . So also, when you see all these things, you know that he is near, at the very gates. Truly, I say to you, this generation will not pass away until all these things take place. (Matt 24:30, 33–34)

Here in Matthew 24, Jesus prepared his original disciples to be ready to personally experience the end of the age events and his return. Again, this did not happen. Was Jesus wrong in his prophetic expectation?

After Paul, the rabbis of the Talmud noted that "all the predestined dates for the redemption have passed, and now the matter only depends on repentance and good deeds" (Tractate Sanhedrin 97b). Here, the rabbis lamented the fact that the redemption did not happen when it could and perhaps should have.

So, what do we make of these unfulfilled prophetic expectations? One answer is that these predictions are plain wrong, with nothing left to discuss. But such an answer would not do justice to the complex components involved when Jewish prophets speak their oracles.

Prophets can present expectations that can *possibly* come to pass but do not due to factors outside their control. This is not a loophole or a back door escape route. It's the arithmetic of biblical prophecy. Simply stated, it goes like this:

Prophecy + Human cooperation = Fulfillment of the prophecy

Human cooperation, responsiveness, and preparedness are fundamental factors built into the equation of biblical prophecy. Abraham Joshua Heschel expresses this concept in his classic book *The Prophets*, "This is the mysterious paradox of the Hebrew faith: The All-wise and Almighty may change a word that He proclaims. Man has the power to modify His design."[55] Heschel's emphasis on man's role in the unfolding of biblical prophecy is underemphasized, but nonetheless central to the Bible's internal principles. How audiences respond to prophetic messages can hasten, delay, and even halt a prophecy from happening.

The prophet Jeremiah expressed how human involvement factors into the outcome of biblical prophecy:

If at any time I declare concerning a nation or a kingdom, that I will pluck up and break down and destroy it, and if that nation, concerning which I have spoken, turns from its evil, I will relent of the disaster that I intended to do to it. And if at any time I declare concerning a nation or a kingdom that I will build and plant it, and if it does evil in my sight, not listening to my voice, then I will relent of the good that I had intended to do to it. Now, therefore, say to the men of Judah and the inhabitants of Jerusalem: "Thus says the Lord, Behold,

I am shaping disaster against you and devising a plan against you. Return, every one from his evil way, and amend your ways and your deeds." (Jer 18:7–11)

According to Jeremiah, a nation or kingdom's orientation away from or toward evil can directly impact prophetic outcomes. And the New Testament book of 2 Peter also communicates with clarity how human behavior can impact prophetic timelines: "Since all these things are thus to be dissolved, what sort of people ought you to be in lives of holiness and godliness, waiting for and hastening the coming of the day of God, because of which the heavens will be set on fire and dissolved, and the heavenly bodies will melt as they burn!" (2 Pet 3:11–12).

According to this text, "the day of God" can be "hastened." Presumably, it can be delayed as well. Clearly, how people conduct themselves significantly influences prophetic results.

Now, back to Paul. His expectations and hopes regarding Jesus's return within his lifetime did not come to pass. But that does not put him out of compliance with the internal principles of how Jewish biblical prophecy works.

Perhaps Paul was correct that the end of the age *could* have happened in his lifetime. How one feels about that is debatable. But the fact that Jesus's return didn't happen in accordance with Paul's expectations doesn't mean we should dismiss him as wrongheaded or misguided. It just means Paul was like other Jewish end-times (eschatological) predictors whose clocks were not synchronized with their prophetic forecasts.

TWO WORDS THAT WILL MAKE YOU LOOK SMART AT A PARTY

As we measure how Paul's weird view of time impacts our understanding of him, there are two distinct yet related keywords we need to discuss. Paul was both *apocalyptic* and *eschatological* in his view of time.

Try dropping those two words at a party. Folks will think you are hot stuff.

More likely, if you drop "apocalyptic" and "eschatological" into a social gathering, even most Bible lovers won't know what in the world (pun intended) you are talking about. But you might get them to lean forward if you say both words have to do with the end of the world as we know it!

In all seriousness, Paul's outlook was shaped by his apocalyptic and eschatological framework as a Jewish man convinced that the messianic, prophetic, end-times clock was now ticking.

But what do these words mean, and how do they relate to Paul?

An apocalyptic Jew believes they are straddling this current age and the ideal, utopian age to come.[56] The word "apocalyptic" has a Greek origin, meaning "unveiling" or "revelatory." David Clausen, a scholar specializing in Christian origins, provides a helpful explanation of the "apocalyptic" literary genre: "An apocalyptic narrative is an account of someone's (visionary) experience that was interpreted for them by a supernatural figure. It often (but not necessarily) reveals something about the end of the world (Greek: *eschaton*). Paul's letters demonstrate that he was an apocalyptic visionary."[57]

The New Testament book of Revelation is a well-known example of Jewish apocalyptic literature. It is chock full of visions, supernatural mediators, and end-of-the-world scenarios. But the book of Revelation and other works widely categorized as apocalyptic are shaped quite differently than Paul's letters. Notwithstanding his "otherworldly" account of a trip to heaven in 2 Corinthians 12:1–10 and apocalyptic expressions peppered throughout his letters, Paul's correspondence remains anchored primarily to questions pertaining to life in this world. Thus, I agree with New Testament scholar Jamie Davies's assessment: "I continue to find it helpful to think of Paul as a writer not of apocalypses but very much in the 'apocalyptic mode.'"[58]

As one in the "apocalyptic mode," Paul boasted of multiple visions and revelations (2 Cor 12:1). In fact, it was because of his many revelations (Greek = *apokalupseon*) that he was given a "thorn in the flesh" to keep him humble (2 Cor 12:7).

Simply put, "apocalyptic" is a fitting term for Paul because his letters include multiple claims that he received visions, revelations, and unveiled information regarding God's redemptive program as the world passed into a new age.

The new utopian age the prophets spoke of had not fully arrived in Paul's mind. But the end of the age was very near. And Paul's sense of that nearness was why we also need to think of Paul in eschatological terms. To start us toward a definition of that fancy word, I'll take you back to a funny moment at my favorite Starbucks across the street.

JERUSALEM SYNDROME AND THE ESCHATOLOGICAL APOSTLE

A few years ago, I was sitting at Starbucks with my dear friend, Doc Littlefield, just days before his first trip to Israel. Because Doc is a medical doctor, I jokingly alerted him to watch out for folks in the holy city with a case of Jerusalem Syndrome. We drew a few stares as Doc's booming laughter shook our table while I described this condition. I had to give Doc a minute. When he settled down, I shared with him that this is a real thing.

Jerusalem Syndrome is rare, but it happens when a person becomes intoxicated with the religious fervor and experience of being in Jerusalem. Jerusalem Syndrome has various manifestations, but it frequently involves individuals in a state of delusion who temporarily believe they are biblical characters such as Jesus, John the Baptist, or a prophet such as Jeremiah. I've seen this happen. And, yes, it's quite a scene.

Sometimes, folks in this state proclaim doomsday messages that the end of the world is about to happen. Typically, people who present such end-times proclamations create a disturbance, but no harm.

We have no evidence of Paul engaging in Jerusalem Syndrome activity involving delusional, psychotic behavior. But he very much operated as an urgent, eschatological figure. His apocalyptic visions led him to believe Jesus's death and resurrection would soon usher in the end of the age and a transition into the era foretold by the Jewish prophets when the kingdom of God would rule the earth.

THE TWO HANDS ON PAUL'S WATCH

"Apocalyptic" and "eschatological" are like the two hands on Paul's watch. Each served to formulate his weird view of time. So, how do these two hands synchronize? Think of "apocalyptic" as the revelations and unveiled visions Paul received, and think of "eschatological" as an outlook about the end of the world in its current form.

Paul's apocalyptic outlook, as informed by multiple visions and revelations, was deeply eschatological (focused on the end-times). In other words, his apocalyptic revelations persuaded him that the end of the age was near.

And here's why this matters: The two hands on Paul's watch deeply affected the nature, tone, and time-sensitive instruction in his letters.

Paul did not consider *our* circumstances when he wrote his letters. It's not that Paul would not have cared about you, me, and our time. He just didn't think there would be you and me. Paul was not even thinking about the generation that would follow him. That's because he was convinced his generation was the final one.

Paul's end-times outlook deeply affected how he crafted his letters and the instructions he offered to his communities. As Paula Fredriksen says, "The theme of the nearness of the End shapes the substance of Paul's pastoral advice."[59]

For Christians, Paul's letters and the instructions therein are timeless. Thus, what the apostle wrote then very much informs what faithfulness looks like now. But here's a key point to remember when applying the words of the Weird Apostle in modern times: The transcendence of Paul's letters does not negate the importance of factoring in his short-term outlook when applying his instructions to a modern audience.

A FAIR BUT DIFFICULT QUESTION

When interpreting Paul, it is important to wrestle with a difficult question: If Paul had known time would march on well beyond his lifetime, might he have expressed himself differently? We don't know. But because of Paul's ongoing prominence and impact, it's an important question to ask as we seek to understand him today.

In 1 Corinthians 10:11, Paul explicitly stated that he believed the end of the ages had come. Thus, it seems sensible that he advised the Corinthians in the following ways:

- Don't engage in sexual activity unless you can't help yourself (1 Cor 7:1–2).
- If you are single, remain single, unless you are burning with passion (1 Cor 7:8).
- Don't seek divorce (1 Cor 7:10–16).

Paul had a wartime mentality. In his mind, the return of the Lord was at hand (Phil 4:5). So these instructions make sense if your time horizon is short. These statements are not nuanced, and they don't consider the many complexities of life. For Paul, the time was too short to be distracted by details like marriage and divorce. That would all be irrelevant when Jesus returned—soon.

But Jesus didn't return during Paul's lifetime. And here's a big reason why that matters: Paul did not knowingly craft his letters for people he believed would have to continue navigating the twists and turns of a full life in the world as we know it, generation after generation.

Thus, for those seeking to apply Paul's letters personally and pastorally, Paul's timelessness should always be balanced with his weird, short-term view of time.

SYMPATHIZING WITH OTHER WATCHES

Before we conclude our discussion on Paul's view of time, it's important to remember that most other Jews were not in sync with how the apostle was reading his watch. They understood his sense of time as not only weird but dangerous.

Because the end of the ages was unfolding, Paul felt it was the right time to receive non-Jews into God's kingdom, as the ancient prophets had predicted. But Paul's Jewish contemporaries were widely in disagreement about what Gentile inclusion in God's kingdom would look like.

Ancient Jewish views varied on the role of non-Jews in the age of utopia. Most Jews in the ancient world probably didn't have a strong opinion about this. But for those who did, one thing was clear: Non-Jews would no longer give allegiance to their native gods.

According to the Jewish prophets, the God of Israel would be worshipped alone in the kingdom of God. The prophet Zechariah expressed this succinctly and clearly: "And the Lord will be king over all the earth. On that day, the Lord will be one and his name one" (Zech 14:9).

Paul believed the time for the conversion of the nations had come. To use Paula Fredriksen's term, Paul's non-Jews were "eschatological Gentiles."[60] And his compressed, urgent view of time, perhaps more than any other factor, is why Paul faced such fierce opposition from multiple directions, especially from his Jewish brethren. The Jewish community was terrified at the prospect of how Paul's time-driven message for non-Jews would affect their standing as a minority population in the Roman empire. Matthew Novenson sums up these implications clearly:

Paul was putting the already vulnerable diaspora Jewish communities at risk from their Gentile neighbors by recruiting Gentiles into his Jewish movement and then teaching them to renounce their obligations to their civic and family gods. This would have looked like Jewish promotion of impiety among Gentiles, an understandable cause of outrage among the locals and a public relations nightmare for synagogue leaders, who would have used the means at their disposal to keep a self-authorized charismatic like Paul in line for the health and safety of the community.[61]

Whether or not one agrees with his sense of time, Paul's apocalyptic, eschatological urgency was understandably not welcomed by those who did not share his conviction in how the death and resurrection of Jesus triggered the commencement of the kingdom of God.

HOW DOES THIS CHANGE THE GAME?

Friday nights at the Lambert house are predictable. But they are far from boring.

My wife and I are Jewish, and a special Shabbat[62] meal is part of our weekly rhythm. After some blessings and a delicious meal, we conclude our Sabbath Table time with a fun and meaningful discussion. Topics can touch on concepts ranging from biblical texts to current events and a whole lot in between. As you can imagine, these discussions get significantly more animated on weekends when the kids are with us.

During a recent Shabbat discussion, we discussed a contemporary, hot-button issue facing American Christianity regarding the ordination of women pastors. In true Lambert style, we debated our various opinions with passion. And as is often the case, some of the kids pushed back on my take—which I welcome. Respectful disagreement is fair game at the Lambert Shabbat Table.

As we exchanged our thoughts, I was reminded that it is largely Paul's letters from which Christians form their opinions on whether women can be ordained as pastors and elders. And one of my big points in the discussion was to be cautious and considerate about how the time-sensitive pastoral instructions in the Pauline epistles apply in a modern context.

Paul had a weird view of time. We can be confident Paul wrote things that, if asked, he would have categorized as timeless. But he also provided instructions based on an apocalyptic, eschatological outlook. Paul thought Jesus was coming back soon, which profoundly shaped his opinions on how life should be lived for himself and his audience.

We don't know how Paul would have thought about ordaining women pastors had he foreseen that Jesus would not return in his lifetime. The fact that the Pauline letters assume male leadership within his Jesus-following assemblies does not require that his letters preclude female leadership for all time. This is a present-day question that Paul, in his time, was not seeking to answer.

Thus, for *both* those who turn to Paul for answers to modern spiritual questions and for those interested in Paul as a historical figure only, it is critical to keep Paul's tight time horizon in mind. That's not easy, considering Paul's letters have circulated for nearly two thousand years. It's a natural default to think Paul was writing to guide Christians for many generations. But he wasn't.

Paul was writing to small subgroups of Judaism, composed primarily of non-Jews, who embraced his good-news message about Jesus. And Paul assured these non-Jews that Jesus was returning very soon. He was not considering the possibility of continuing to have an audience beyond the people receiving his letters.

But history did not unfold in accord with Paul's watch. Thus, it's a game changer to read and interpret Paul's letters by remembering that he did not write his letters for you, me, or any generation beyond his own. Doing so is unfamiliar and odd for most readers of Paul. But remembering Paul's weird view of time will help avoid various misunderstandings about the man, his letters, and how his instructions can be applied to modern audiences.

GAME-CHANGING ACTION

When I attend the Society of Biblical Literature (SBL)[63] each year, I am continually intrigued by the multitude of angles in which the Bible is researched. Frameworks for studying, interpreting, and applying the biblical text vary widely. There are Jewish groups. Christians groups. Feminist groups. African American groups. LGBTQ groups. Somewhere within each of these groups, to varying degrees, you will find those who seek to understand Paul within their respective outlook.

Regardless of one's framework or angle for engaging with the Weird Apostle, it is critical to remember that his sensibilities as a Christ-follower were shaped by a firm commitment to the Torah and his ongoing identity as a Pharisee. An often ignored, yet indispensable, consideration in understanding Paul is his weird, short-term view of time. And here's a game-changing question to ask when reading and seeking to understand his letters: Is it possible Paul would have communicated this instruction differently if he had known time would continue well into the future?

This question is particularly important for those who view Paul as an authoritative, apostolic figure. And this is not an easy question to ask. It is far easier to assume that how Paul put it then is how he would put it now—especially for those who value his letters as holy Scripture. After all, if Paul's letters are God's word, then the message is timeless, right? Well, "timeless" and "time-sensitive" are two different things. And considering both in applying Paul's letters to a modern audience requires considerable dynamic engagement with both Paul's words and current times.

Trying to figure out Paul's view on a particular issue is not merely a matter of what he wrote in his letters. Perhaps Paul would have thought differently about certain topics if he felt he had more time. Thus, those interested in trying to discern Paul's view on a matter—regardless of the space one is doing so within—will do well to do the hard work of not only analyzing what he wrote but also considering his view of time.

Paul's small corpus of letters contains some of the most influential literature ever penned. But the Weird Apostle's letters had an influence of their own, something not frequently considered: Paul did not expect time to keep moving unrelentingly.

CHAPTER 6

Paul's Weird Lifestyle, Part 1

Paul's something against the wind

The *Weird Apostle* soundtrack may be a better idea than the book. There are no plans for a soundtrack. But it would be chock full of hits!

Yes, many of my examples, stories, and illustrations are based on songs. Most people get this. Songs have a powerful way of connecting our emotions and memories. They are also handy for helping to introduce or push points along.

So, get ready. Another one is coming.

SOMETHING AGAINST THE WIND

It only takes a nudge to get me thinking, reflecting, and sometimes talking about lessons I've learned from both victories and losses in my life. My wife insists I should write a book about how to recover, learn, and grow after experiencing deep disappointment and failure.

Life is brutal at times, and my life has had its share of such moments. I'm not unique in the challenges I've experienced, but maybe Kara is right that I do have something helpful to share. I've learned some things about how to be resilient and turn failures and disappointment into opportunities for growth and improvement. If I do write the book Kara wants me to write, I know at least one big point I will share: the value of "home."

When I speak of home, I'm not exclusively referring to a physical structure. In my outlook, home stands for special people, truths, and places that are a refuge and safe place when life kicks you in the tail. My observation is that life without a home will leave you exposed and vulnerable when—not *if*—you need to grab an anchor that will hold.

Yes, the most difficult and dangerous way to experience life's hurricanes is if we don't have shelters to hunker down when we need some safety, protection, and peace. Bob Seger expressed this powerfully in his 1980 hit song "Against the Wind." This song describes a familiar human journey. When we are young, we feel strong and independent. We are invincible and ready to run headlong into the wind. But as time passes, things change. We tend to start pursuing stability and anchors that ground us and give us a sense of belonging. We start looking for a cover from the wind.

The shelter Seger longs for is much more than bricks and concrete. He's longing for an anchor, a safe place, or a safe relationship—a home he can count on. Home is something, someone, or someplace that's a sure thing—that you don't lose faith in and doesn't lose faith in you—in both the best and worst of times.

Everyone needs something against the wind.

PAUL'S SHELTER

I wonder if Paul had something against the wind?

Being a prominent leader in a thriving movement can be lonely, even in good times. But Paul wrote that times were not always good. His life as an apostle included a long list of difficulties. One of Paul's trials included challenges to his authority as an apostle. During a defense of his credentials in one of his letters to the Christ-followers in Corinth, he said:

> I am talking like a madman—with far greater labors, far more imprisonments, with countless beatings, and often near death. Five times I received at the hands of the Jews the forty lashes less one. Three times I was beaten with rods. Once I was stoned. Three times I was shipwrecked; a night and a day I was adrift at sea; on frequent journeys, in danger from rivers, danger from robbers, danger from my own people, danger from Gentiles, danger in the city, danger in the wilderness, danger at sea, danger from false brothers; in toil and hardship, through many a sleepless night, in hunger and thirst, often without food, in cold and exposure. And, apart from other things, there is the daily pressure on me of my anxiety for all the churches. Who is weak, and I am not weak? (2 Cor 11:23–29)

If anyone needed a little something against the wind, Paul did.

But, I wonder, what was his refuge? Did he have friends he could turn to? Special places? What was his anchor? I'm confident Paul ran to God when he was in trouble. We see that in his letters; that certainly comforted him. But I'm not sure how Paul would answer those questions himself.

Paul hinted that he possibly had people and places that gave him a taste of home. He mentioned a few names he may have considered friends, like Barnabas and Timothy. And at one point, he "went away into Arabia" (Gal 1:17), so perhaps Paul had his sources of refuge where he could vent and be "off" for a bit.

But there was another fundamental aspect to Paul that anchored him his entire life. This grounding force was not a person or a place, but rather a home base that went with him in every direction the wind blew. This identity marker continually reminded him who he was and how he should live in this world—both before and after his flash moment on the Damascus Road.

The wisdom and guidance of the Torah served as a refuge and guiding light for Paul until his last breath.

PAUL AND CHANGING WINDS

For most Christians and Jews, it's close to impossible to imagine the Apostle Paul as a Torah-observant Jew. And it's not difficult to figure out why. Pamela Eisenbaum nails it regarding the difficulty in perceiving Paul in such terms:

> Readers have largely presumed that Paul's embrace of Christ necessarily involves a rejection of Torah, and so they have read his letters through this lens. Because a Christian is defined as someone who has faith in Jesus, while a Jew is defined as someone who puts their faith in Torah, Torah observance and faith in Jesus are assumed to be mutually exclusive.[64]

The non-Jewish, non-Torah-observant Paul is reinforced in every form in which Paul is shaped, including art. From Rembrandt to the statue of Paul in front of St. Peter's Basilica in Rome, I know of zero artistic renderings of the Weird Apostle that include identifiable Jewish features. He is persistently depicted as Saint Paul the Christian.

Even the cover of Matthew Thiessen's excellent book *A Jewish Paul*[65] depicts Paul with a not-so-Jewish look. But we shouldn't blame Thiessen. To my knowledge, public depictions of a Jewish-looking Paul do not exist.[66] And that's because the artistic compositions of Paul have consistently reflected the prevailing narrative regarding Paul's lifestyle, a narrative that generally goes like this: Paul lived as a Torah-observant, Jewish Pharisee within Judaism before he became a Christian. Once he converted to Christianity, his Jewish identity became irrelevant and he no longer lived according to the Torah, except when it was useful for evangelistic purposes.

Tom Schreiner, a prominent Christian scholar, emphasizes the mainstream Christian view of Paul's lifestyle in relation to the Torah and Judaism:

> Paul's desire to bring the gospel to the Gentiles, without forsaking a witness to the Jews, explains his flexibility relative to the law. . . . When he was with the Jews only he practiced Jewish customs and the law to bring the Jews to faith in Christ. But when he was with Gentiles he abandoned Jewish distinctives, such as observance of food and purity laws, in order to win Gentiles for the gospel of Christ.[67]

Essentially, Schreiner is saying Paul kept the Torah only when it was expedient to do so—namely, when he was evangelizing Jews. Schreiner's view is standard.

But recently, a growing number of Christian and Jewish scholars have faced the prevailing winds head-on by challenging deeply anchored assumptions about Paul's lifestyle. And in fact, the wind itself is beginning to shift regarding Paul and his relation to Judaism. It is no longer a given that Paul, as an apostle, departed from Judaism and the Torah.

A wave is slowly building that advances the idea that rather than becoming a law-free Christian, Paul continued living as a Torah-observant, Judaism-keeping Jew. This means Paul celebrated the Sabbath and Jewish holidays, worshiped in the Jerusalem Temple, and observed the Jewish dietary laws—even among Gentiles.

If Paul continued keeping the Torah and assumed other Jews would do the same, a very untraditional portrait of Paul emerges. Such a picture of Paul would be pretty weird to most of us—with various implications for how we view Paul's lifestyle and understand his letters.

One would be this: At my imaginary meeting with Paul at From the Earth, the Weird Apostle would not order the Italian Grinder Salad—with its hearty dose of ham, pepperoni, and salami! I've seen folks down that salad plenty of times—and it looks amazing—but it wouldn't work for Paul. As a passionate follower of Jesus, Paul continued living Jewishly, within Judaism, and according to the Torah. That meant eating kosher food only.[68] No ham, pepperoni, or (non-kosher) salami for the Weird Apostle.

Listen, I understand. A Torah-free Paul is more familiar to most of us. Perhaps that's a Paul who is more relatable. And, you might think, it's a Paul you could have over for dinner.

Rest assured, Torah-observing Paul could still come over to your house for dinner. Considering his intensity, I'm not sure he would be the most enjoyable dinner guest, but, theoretically, it could be done.[69] However, it would require you to provide food consistent with the Torah's kosher dietary requirements.

Paul had a weird lifestyle. As a follower of Jesus, he kept the Torah. Naturally, this raises one of my favorite questions: Why?

Why did Paul keep the Torah? Let's get into it.

START WITH WHY . . . NORMALLY

I enjoy watching TED Talks. These short, inspirational videos frequently challenge my assumptions and help me think in new and better ways. One such video was one of the first TED Talks I watched, Simon Sinek's "Start With Why."[70]

Sinek's talk and book of the same title emphasize the importance of both individuals and organizations understanding the "why" behind their "what." He says, "Very few people or companies can clearly articulate *why* they do what they do. . . . By *why*, I mean what is your purpose, cause, or belief? . . . Why do you get out of bed every morning? And *why* should anyone care?"[71]

"Why" is a critical starting question for every movement, organization, and person. And the why behind Paul's weird lifestyle is an important question we need to discuss.

But before we get to Paul's why, I will deviate from Sinek's pattern and start broadly with the Apostle's "what." So, why are we starting with what?

Because Paul is the Weird Apostle! What other reason do we need to go out of order?

Seriously, here's why we need to start with Paul's what before exploring his why. For most of the past two thousand years, the what of Paul's lifestyle as a follower of Jesus was a given: Paul left Judaism, no longer lived according to the Torah, and became a "law-free" Christian who did Jewish things only when it helped him be a better evangelist when he was targeting Jews.

But that view of Paul's what is no longer a given. A growing number of modern thinkers believe Paul's lifestyle, as weird as it might sound, was characterized by a firm commitment to keeping the Torah, within Judaism, as a follower of Jesus and as the apostle to the Gentiles.

I hear my mother's voice: "Oy vey, is this guy Paul complicated? And, Ry, you're not making it any easier!" Hang on, Ma. Yes, he's complicated. But bear with me a little longer.

PAUL'S DISPUTED WHAT

Some statements in Paul's letters can create the impression that he left Judaism and no longer lived according to the precepts of the Torah. A well-known text frequently referenced to support the idea that Paul no longer kept the Torah as a consistent way of life is 1 Corinthians 9:20–23:

For though I am free from all, I have made myself a servant to all, that I might win more of them. To the Jews I became as a Jew, in order to win Jews. To those under the law I became as one under the law (though not being myself under the law) that I might win those under the law. To those outside the law I became as one outside the law (not being outside the law of God but under the law of Christ) that I might win those outside the law. To the weak I became weak, that I might win the weak. I have become all things to all people, that by all means I might save some. I do it all for the sake of the gospel, that I may share with them in its blessings.

This is just one of multiple Pauline texts interpreters have understood to mean that Paul developed a loose, expedient, and even negative attitude toward the Torah once he became a follower of Jesus. Again, Schreiner's comments reflect the prevailing viewpoint, which assumes Paul had a shifty relationship with the Torah as a Christ-follower:

For cultural reasons, he [Paul] kept the law when he was with the Jews for the sake of their salvation. . . . But if the situation permitted it, Paul would alter his observance of the Torah, depending on whether he was with Jews or Gentiles. This "inconsistency" in practice promoted a higher goal and aim: to reach as many people as possible with the saving message of the gospel.[72]

But there's a big problem with Schreiner's statement and the standard narrative regarding Paul's departure from Judaism and the Torah as a consistent way of life. Consider the following Torah-positive statements in Paul's letter to the Romans:

- "Then what advantage has the Jew? Or what is the value of circumcision? Much in every way. To begin with, the Jews were entrusted with the oracles of God" (Rom 3:1–2).

- "Do we then overthrow the law by this faith? By no means! On the contrary, we uphold the law" (Rom 3:31).

- "What then shall we say? That the law is sin? By no means!" (Rom 7:7).

- "So the law is holy, and the commandment is holy and righteous and good" (Rom 7:12).

- "They are Israelites, and to them belong the adoption, the glory, the covenants, the giving of the law, the worship, and the promises" (Rom 9:4).

These passages, and many others in the Pauline corpus, led the historian John G. Gager to conclude, "It is simply impossible to reconcile these passages with the view of Paul as the founder of Christian anti-Judaism."[73] Gager's take on these verses from Romans is important to consider. How could someone who was supposedly against Judaism and the Torah make such statements? According to Gager, they couldn't.

The text from 1 Corinthians 9 and other statements in Paul's letters seem quite negative toward the Torah. How do those statements reconcile with these Romans verses? Yes, Paul wrote some things about the Torah in his letters that are hard to understand. But before we get there, I want to briefly share two more important texts as we work our way further into this discussion about Paul's weird lifestyle—and the why behind it.

Upon returning to Jerusalem from one of his apostolic journeys, Acts 21 records chatter among the Jewish Christ-followers that Paul was teaching and living in a way that represented a desertion of the Torah. But the leaders of the Jerusalem assembly, headed by James, spoke up and squashed these rumors:

You see, brother, how many thousands there are among the Jews of those who have believed. They are all zealous for the law, **and they have been told about you that you teach all the Jews who are among the Gentiles to forsake Moses,**

telling them not to circumcise their children or walk according to our customs. What then is to be done? They will certainly hear that you have come. Do therefore what we tell you. We have four men who are under a vow; take these men and purify yourself along with them and pay their expenses, so that they may shave their heads. **Thus all will know that there is nothing in what they have been told about you, but that you yourself also live in observance of the law**. But as for the Gentiles who have believed, we have sent a letter with our judgment that they should abstain from what has been sacrificed to idols, and from blood, and from what has been strangled, and from sexual immorality. (Acts 21:20–25)

A lot is going on in this text. For now, let's focus on one big point. According to these Jerusalem-based leaders in the first generation of the Jesus movement, Paul lived "in observance of the law." In their minds, despite rumors to the contrary, Paul's lifestyle as a Torah-observant Jew was unassailable.

Later in Acts, Luke described another scene affirming Paul's consistent Torah observance as an apostle. Upon arriving in Rome as a prisoner, Paul requested the local Jewish leaders to visit him. When they gathered, he testified to the following:

After three days he called together the local leaders of the Jews, and when they had gathered, he said to them, "Brothers, **though I had done nothing against our people or the customs of our fathers**, yet I was delivered as a prisoner from Jerusalem into the hands of the Romans. When they had examined me, they wished to set me at liberty, because there was no reason for the death penalty in my case. But because the Jews objected, I was compelled to appeal to Caesar—though I had no charge to bring against my nation. For this reason, therefore, I have asked to see you and speak with you, since it is because of the hope of Israel that I am wearing this chain." (Acts 28:17–20)

The significance of Paul's statement that he "had done nothing against our people or the customs of our fathers" is easy to breeze past. But it is an essential detail regarding what the author of Acts understood about Paul's view of his lifestyle. Doing nothing against "our people" and "the customs of our fathers" is a Jewish way of saying that Paul's Torah observance was beyond repute.

So, what do we do now? How did this guy live? What was Paul's what?

Did the Torah continue being an anchor and lifestyle guide for the Apostle Paul, as Acts seems to indicate? Or do Paul's letters present an apostle who made a break from the Torah as a consistent way of life?

THE CLARITY OF PAUL'S WHAT IN ACTS

I plan to look closer at the nature of Paul's (weird) letters in the next book in this series. For now, I'll highlight a critical point about the relationship between Paul's letters and Acts that is crucial to understanding his weird lifestyle. Actually, I'll let the excellent Pauline scholar Isaac Oliver make the point for me:

Whereas the situational and rhetorical nature of Paul's letters may convey the impression that Paul forsook or became indifferent about his Jewish heritage, Acts clarified that Paul continued to view himself as a Jew well after his unique encounter with the risen Christ on his way to Damascus. . . . In Acts, Paul never speaks disparagingly of the Torah. Paul only opposed the circumcision of Gentiles. Otherwise, he continued to uphold the observance of the Torah for Jews.[74]

In Acts, Paul's what is clear. As a follower of Jesus, he kept the Torah. And, as Oliver sees it, "It seems likely that Acts was written precisely to counter the rumors circulating among Jewish followers of Jesus and Jews in general that Paul was an apostate."[75] An apostate, from a Jewish standpoint in Paul's time, was someone who fell away from or neglected Torah observance. I agree with Oliver that the author of Acts was determined to demonstrate that the Weird Apostle was no such Jew.

Throughout Acts, the Torah anchored Paul. It served as the foundation for his life as a man of God. It was a little something against the wind. His Torah faithfulness is wound seamlessly through the book:

- In Acts 16:3, Paul had the Jewish Timothy circumcised, thus upholding one of the fundamental observances of the Torah.
- In Acts 18:18, Paul took a Nazirite vow (see Num 6:1–21), another sacred Torah ritual, demonstrating a commitment to purity and holiness.
- In Acts 20:16, Paul reportedly hurried back to Jerusalem in time to celebrate Pentecost (Hebrew: *Shavuot*), a holiday instituted in the Torah (Lev 23) associated with the giving of the Torah.
- In Acts 21:17–26, Paul went through great trouble and expense to pay the costs associated with the Torah-prescribed "Nazirite vows" for several men—thus countering rumors in Jerusalem that questioned his fidelity to the Torah.
- In Acts 23:6, Paul stated in the *present* tense that he was a Pharisee—an unmistakable identification with a Torah way of life.
- In Acts 24:17–18, while speaking to the Roman governor Felix, Paul declared he brought alms and offerings to the Temple in Jerusalem.

This cluster of texts from Acts leads Pauline scholar David Rudolph to say, "One may ask what more Luke could have included in his narrative to express that Paul was a Torah observant Jew."[76]

And the last text in that list is fascinating—with broad and deep implications. How interesting that Acts presents two accounts (21:17–26 and 24:17–18) that associate Paul, as a follower of Jesus, with offering Torah-defined sacrifices in the Jerusalem Temple. Later Christian theology viewed the sacrifice and priesthood of Jesus as replacing the Torah's sacrificial and priestly system. Paul did not seem to share this view. According to Acts, Paul's what as a follower of Jesus included regular trips to the Temple in Jerusalem—to pray and offer Levitical, Torah-defined sacrifices.

Yes, that sounds a little weird. Suppose Paul had an iPhone in his day. I imagine we would find photos of him in Jerusalem—and perhaps even selfies of him worshipping and presenting offerings—in the Jerusalem Temple. Maybe that's pushing it too far. But you get the point.

It's difficult for us to imagine a picture of Paul worshipping and presenting offerings in the temple. But it is how Acts frames him. Nonetheless, you will be hard-pressed to find artwork (or biblical commentaries) depicting such a view of Paul.

But Paul had a weird lifestyle. As a Torah-observant Jewish man, he worshipped regularly in the Jerusalem Temple. The Weird Apostle did not appear to feel conflict between his allegiance to Jesus and the activities in the temple. For him, the temple offerings and sacrifices complemented but did not compete with the atoning work of Jesus.

PAUL'S SPECIAL PLACE

Let's dial in on this idea of Paul and the Jerusalem Temple. Many commentators sweep this segment of biblical data under the rug, but this is way too big of an issue to do that.

Traditional thinking goes something like this: Jesus replaced the temple. His sacrifice replaced the animal sacrifices. Therefore, the temple and all the confusing stuff about priests and sacrifices in Leviticus became irrelevant.

But there is a problem with that viewpoint. In the New Testament, Acts in particular, Paul was closely connected to the temple. Why was this? Why, according to Acts, did Paul seem so drawn to the temple?

Perhaps Paul viewed the temple as something against the wind. Maybe he saw it as a refuge and a place to draw near to God. That's a weird thought—for us. But it would have been ordinary for a Torah-observant Jewish man like Paul to see the Jerusalem Temple as a special place. And that place continues to draw people close and provides an extraordinary sense of awe, inspiration, and peace. I like to think of this pull on Paul, and countless others both then and now, as the "the makom magnetism."

THE MAKOM MAGNETISM

In the Torah, Jerusalem was not yet defined as the holy city where the temple would be built. At that point, the house for God's presence and the sacrificial system were conducted in the traveling holy place known as the Tabernacle (Hebrew: *Mishkan*). However, the Torah anticipated that a *makom*, a place, would be fixed where God's name would dwell and sacrifices would be offered.

Later in the Bible, the temple was built in Jerusalem through the efforts of King David and his son Solomon. Since then, Jerusalem and the Temple Mount have served as the geographical and spiritual epicenter for the Jewish people.

Most Christian theological viewpoints include a diminished view of the significance of Jerusalem and the temple. However, in recent times, more commentators and scholars are alternatively emphasizing the centrality of Jerusalem and the temple in the New Testament.[77]

These scholars highlight that Paul returned to the temple repeatedly and brought sacrifices—even as an apostle.

A temple-loving Paul may not fit well into how the apostle is typically understood, but that image is consistent with multiple New Testament texts we have already noted. This is a game changer in how Paul, the New Testament, and the first followers of Jesus are understood.

Paul and the first followers of Jesus continued seeing the temple as the *Beit HaMikdash*, the holy house. It was a spiritual home they kept returning to. It was their *makom*, their place.

The city of Jerusalem and its temple had a magnetic effect on Paul. This is a force I can relate to. Allow me to share something personal, a bit mystical, and, some may say, weird. I promise I'll bring it back to Paul. But this thing about the temple is extremely important as we discuss Paul's lifestyle, Jerusalem, the temple . . . and a little something against the wind.

THE KOTEL

I've been to Israel many times. Every hill in the Holy Land has a story, but there is something unique about the city of Jerusalem. The city's spiritual essence is palpable. A diverse range of people experience this difficult-to-quantify energy—regardless of the faith or even doubts one brings with them to the holy city. And for many, things get stranger and more difficult to explain within the Old City of Jerusalem.

Once inside the city walls, it's not unusual to sense a mystical pull to a place, a *makom*, that I can only describe as magnetic—especially by the Western Wall. The Western Wall—or Wailing Wall, as some call it—is the lone intact remnant from the last standing Jewish temple, which was destroyed by the Romans in 70 AD. The Kotel, as the Western Wall is referred to in Hebrew, is the holiest site in Judaism. It serves as a place of worship, hope, and inspiration.

At the Kotel, it feels like home. It's a place where I feel close to God. Clarity, peace, and creativity flow for me there—especially at night. Despite being one of the most controversial pieces of real estate on the planet, I feel safe there. That's all I can explain about the Kotel's makom magnetism. For me, it's real.

And there are indications that Jerusalem and the temple had a comparable effect on Paul. It was a little something against the wind for him. That's because for Paul, his what as a follower of Jesus remained intimately connected to the Torah. Acts makes that clear.

But what is evident in Acts about Paul's weird lifestyle as a Torah-observant Jew is *less* evident in his letters—which raise some critical questions about the what and why of Paul's lifestyle.

PAUL'S VAGUE WHAT IN HIS LETTERS

While Acts provides abundant evidence that Paul's what can be characterized as a Torah-observant follower of Jesus, his letters are less clear. In fact, his letters not only raise questions about his fidelity to the Torah, but they can come across as hostile to the Torah. The following statements from Paul's letters have led interpreters to conclude that Paul's lifestyle departed from Judaism and the Torah:

- "For in Christ Jesus neither circumcision nor uncircumcision counts for anything, but only faith working through love" (Gal 5:6).
- "But now we are released from the law, having died to that which held us captive, so that we serve in the new way of the Spirit and not in the old way of the written code" (Rom 7:6).
- "Therefore let no one pass judgment on you in questions of food and drink, or with regard to a festival or a new moon or a Sabbath. These are a shadow of the things to come, but the substance belongs to Christ" (Col 2:16–17).

- "Do you not know that you are God's temple and that God's Spirit dwells in you? If anyone destroys God's temple, God will destroy him. For God's temple is holy, and you are that temple" (1 Cor 3:16–17).

These do not sound like statements from a person who continued upholding the Torah for himself or others. They sound more like they are coming from a person who once was part of Judaism but no longer is.

These texts, and others like them in Paul's letters, have led to a broad consensus among Christians and Jews that Paul left Judaism. Based on his letters, the following seems clear about Paul: He was against circumcision. He viewed the Holy Spirit as replacing the role of the Torah. He viewed the Jewish Sabbath and festivals as outdated. He viewed the community of Christ-followers as a replacement for the Jerusalem Temple.

We will dial in on each of those ideas (and the texts they are based on) soon. But first, let's make sure we are clear on the big picture.

Historically, it has been almost universally assumed that the what of Paul's lifestyle no longer included consistent Torah observance. And the Torah certainly was not a refuge for him—or a little something against the wind. Instead, Paul is understood to have been set free from the bondage of the Torah.

Now, at this point, some might respond, "Wait a minute . . . you're taking this too far! We know Paul talked about keeping God's commandments. And he even said that the law is good. It's over in Romans that he said, concerning the Torah, 'The law is holy, and the commandment is holy and righteous and good' (Rom 7:12). I'll also remind you Paul continued to emphatically identify as a Jew (Rom 11:1–2; 2 Cor 11:22; Phil 3:5–6)."

Yes, some aim to balance this discussion by noting that Paul made some pro-Torah statements in his letters. And it's widely acknowledged that he said things that affirmed his ethnicity as a Jew. As one Bible teacher with a huge platform once told me, "Paul never got over being a Jew."

Umm . . . I wasn't exactly sure how to take that comment. But this teacher meant that Paul didn't *entirely* do away with being Jewish—although he should have (in her mind).

So, here's the bottom line of where things are on both a popular and academic level when it comes to Paul's lifestyle: Most everyone acknowledges Paul's Jewishness. But the real question is, what kind of Jew was he?

If you spend enough time analyzing Paul's interpreters, you will find that most sum up his lifestyle with some variation of the following: Paul continued identifying as a Jew but didn't practice much Judaism or Torah anymore.

Respected Pauline scholar John Barclay puts it like this:

> Paul took his life in Christ to be governed no longer by the traditions of (what he calls) "Judaism," even though he continues to call himself a "Jew" . . . identifies with his people . . . and finds the "Jewish" Scriptures resonant with the echoes of the good news. As a believer, Paul is a "Jew" who (in his terms) no longer remains "in Judaism."[78]

According to Barclay and many others, Paul called himself a Jew but didn't practice Judaism anymore. This is tough to wrap my mind around. But here's how I've come to understand the way most folks view Paul's relationship to the Torah: Paul loved and kept the law, and he continued identifying as a Jew . . . he just didn't love and keep Shabbat, Jewish holidays, circumcision, or temple worship anymore once he became a follower of Jesus.

I should be totally serious here. But I do find that humorous. It would be like saying my mom adored the Beatles (which she did) . . . but could do without John, Paul, and Ringo. Now, my mom also loved

George Harrison—the least well-known of the band. But is there really anything resembling the Beatles without John, Paul, and Ringo?

It's incoherent to affirm that Paul kept God's commandments, identified as a Jew, and loved his people while also saying Paul no longer affirmed and personally kept circumcision, Shabbat, Jewish holidays, and worship in the Jerusalem Temple. But this is the dominant view of Paul's lifestyle. And it's why some have labeled Paul as inconsistent, incoherent, and untrustworthy.

So, we need to address some perception problems regarding Paul's lifestyle. Again, his letters seem to be at odds with Acts because of numerous statements suggesting he was indifferent at best, and hostile at worst, toward the Torah and Judaism.

THE WHAT OF PAUL'S LETTERS

Sometimes, solutions to big problems are less complicated than we think. And that's the case here.

Yes, in his letters, Paul made some Torah-negative statements. But here's the key: Paul was not against the Torah for himself, for his fellow Jews, or in general.

Instead, Paul was against those who imposed the Torah on his non-Jewish converts and insisted they needed to become Jews and keep the Torah fully in order to be justified members of God's people.

This is big. This point is a huge crossroads when it comes to how we view the Weird Apostle. Understanding how Paul addressed and advocated for ex-pagan Gentiles to join the Jewish Jesus movement *as non-Jews* is critical to not misreading the apostle's arguments.

So, was Paul against circumcision, the Torah, Jewish holidays, and the Jerusalem Temple? Did he consider those things to be replaced by new and better Christ-centered realities? Let's consider these questions one by one.

~

PAUL AND CIRCUMCISION: YES OR NO?

Yes, Paul was against circumcision. That's where most of Paul's interpreters stop. That's what's familiar.

But we're missing something big, and a little strange, if we don't add a clause to the answer to this question: Yes, Paul was against circumcision *for Gentiles who had become followers of Jesus.*

A central claim of Paul's gospel was that Christ-following Gentiles are fully justified without undergoing *conversion*, which, for males, was symbolized by the physical act of circumcision. Through Christ, Paul proclaimed, non-Jews could become members of equal standing within the people of God.

For the most part, though, this specific sense in which Paul was against circumcision has been obscured in favor of the view that Paul was universally opposed to circumcision. This aspect of Paul's lifestyle and teaching is in dire need of being made weird again.

Paul most certainly was *not* against circumcision for Jews. He was very much for it. In Romans 3:1 he said, "Then what advantage has the Jew? *Or what is the value of circumcision? Much in every way.* To begin with, the Jews were entrusted with the oracles of God."

In chapters 8 and 9, we will dig deeper into Paul's emphasis on the protection of both Jewish and Gentile identities within the ekklesia (church)—which, for Jews, means circumcision must also be protected and encouraged.

For now, here is what's important about Paul's stance on circumcision in his letters: Paul absolutely affirmed the ongoing role of circumcision for Jews. Circumcision is the defining, fundamental mark God appointed (for males) as the sign of Jewish identity (Gen 17:1–14). It was and remains the physical, symbolic act that designates the unique covenantal status of the Jewish people. If Paul did away with circumcision for Jews, then he was doing away with the Jews altogether. And he was not doing that.

Paul's negativity toward circumcision was very specific. Paul was negative toward the idea that Gentiles could obtain a justified standing before God by going through the rite of circumcision—which is symbolic of proselyte conversion to Judaism. This snippet from Paul's letter to the Galatians gets to the heart of Paul's concern:

> Look: I, Paul, say to you that if you accept circumcision, Christ will be of no advantage to you. I testify again to every man who accepts circumcision that he is obligated to keep the whole law. You are severed from Christ, you who would be justified by the law; you have fallen away from grace. For through the Spirit, by faith, we ourselves eagerly wait for the hope of righteousness. For in Christ Jesus neither circumcision nor uncircumcision counts for anything, but only faith working through love. (Gal 5:2–6)

That text, arguably, is what positioned Paul to be one of the most powerful game changers of all time. Paul told *Gentiles* they did not have to become Jews via the rite of circumcision to experience God's grace and a righteous standing before their Creator. It is Christ and the Spirit that justify these ex-pagans. In that sense, in Paul's letters, "neither circumcision nor uncircumcision counts for anything, but only faith [in Christ] working through love."

Understanding the specific, narrow target of Paul's anti-circumcision statements also helps clear up some other questions.

DID PAUL SEE THE HOLY SPIRIT AS SUPERSEDING THE ROLE OF THE TORAH?

We noted before that it kind of sounds like Paul viewed the Holy Spirit as replacing the Torah (a.k.a. "the written code") in Romans 7:6 when he wrote, "we serve in the new way of the Spirit and not in the old way of the written code."

Again, Paul was not making a universal Torah-negating statement here. Paul was writing to Gentiles in Rome. And in these very early stages of the Jesus movement, Paul had to establish fundamental, groundbreaking ideas for non-Jews to clarify their new identity and place within the family of God. One of those ideas was that their standing was complete because in-Christ Gentiles now, mystically, were given new natures via being personally indwelled by the Spirit of God. This broad, unprecedented, and prophetic working of the Holy Spirit was "the new way" to get used to—for both Gentiles and Jews. And that new thing transformed Gentiles from standing condemned and captive as pagans into justified men and women who had been made holy members of God's family alongside Jews.

It was their allegiance to Jesus and their new Spirit-infused nature ("the new way of the Spirit"), not circumcision and Torah observance ("the old way of the written code"), that secured the standing of Paul's Jesus-following Gentiles. Again, it's not hard to misread this stuff and conclude that Paul's specific Torah-negative statements are to be understood generally.

Another big issue here—which I plan to explore more in my next book—is that Paul frequently used collective pronouns such as "we" and "us" rhetorically to make points for his Gentile audience that didn't necessarily apply to him and his fellow Jews in the same way. This is comparable to when I say to my kids, "We've got a lot of homework to get done before we watch the Braves game tonight." It's not my homework that needs to be done. Instead, I am speaking collectively and rhetorically to make a point that doesn't directly apply to me personally.

If we put these statements in Paul's letters in their situational context, the anti-Torah Paul begins to vanish. We see Paul's what was very Torah-centric. A different picture of Paul emerges. It's a Paul who loved and kept the Torah. But it's also a Paul who was nuanced and careful in establishing the identity of in-Christ Gentiles who were adopting Jewish ways of life into their outlook and actions.

DID PAUL MINIMIZE THE SIGNIFICANCE OF THE SABBATH AND JEWISH HOLIDAYS IN HIS LETTERS?

By now, you probably know where I'm going with this answer.

Earlier, I referenced a text in Colossians that, historically, has been interpreted as a denigration by Paul of the Jewish Sabbath and holidays: "Therefore let no one pass judgment on you in questions of food and drink, or with regard to a festival or a new moon or a Sabbath. These are a shadow of the things to come, but the substance belongs to Christ" (Col 2:16–17).

The *ESV Study Bible* reflects what most commentators conclude about these verses: "Christians are no longer obligated to observe OT dietary laws ('food and drink') or festivals, holidays, and special days ('a festival . . . New Moon . . . Sabbath,' Col 2:16), for what these things foreshadowed has been fulfilled in Christ."[79]

Years ago, a pastor of a prominent, highly respected church in Atlanta told me, point blank, that he would never allow a Jewish holiday to be publicly affirmed or celebrated at his church because he saw such practices as "a threat to the gospel" based on Colossians 2:16–17. The pastor expressed the standard view that observing Jewish "shadows" threatens devotion to Christ, who is the substance. I am reluctant to label such a position as anti-Semitic, but I do think the pastor's words reflected a strong anti-Judaism sentiment.

Most Christians, leaders or otherwise, are not so bold and defined in their anti-Judaism. But, reflexively, many Christians and Jews agree Paul had no place for Jewish observances such as Shabbat and Jewish holidays.

But was that Paul's point in Colossians 2? Or was that his point in Galatians? There, he somewhat angrily told his Gentile Christ-followers, "You observe days and months and seasons and years! I am afraid I may have labored over you in vain" (Gal 4:10–11).

Again, this is not a difficult problem to solve—*if* we read Paul's letters within the context of their overall purpose and the specific issues addressed in each letter.

In Colossians, Paul responded to what he understood to be a local, specific threat to the Gentile Christ-following community in Colossae. While it's hard to pinpoint the precise nature of the threat, Paul mentioned details suggesting the Colossians were being influenced to veer from Christ in favor of a syncretistic religious philosophy that included some Jewish elements.

In the flow of Colossians 2, Paul also alerted his audience to non-Jewish elements that could lead them astray, such as asceticism (or severe self-denial) and "worship of angels." Whoever this group(s) is Paul was concerned about, they were not advancing a decisively Jewish agenda. As Christian commentator Lionel Windsor notes:

> Several interpreters take this text to mean that Christ has abolished the Jewish ritual elements of the law of Moses for all people (including for Jewish believers in Christ). However, this conclusion is unwarranted. . . . It is far more likely that this is a list of practices adopted by the syncretistic religious philosophy, which had incorporated Jewish elements, among others, and which poses a threat to the Colossians' faith in Christ.[80]

I wish we had more information about what was happening with Paul's non-Jews in Colossae. What's clear is that Paul was concerned the Colossians would depart from their allegiance to Christ in favor of, in his mind, an unhealthy philosophical path that included a blend of Jewish and pagan elements.

I see multiple ways to interpret Colossians 2:16–17, including the possibility that Paul was *encouraging* Gentiles to include Jewish practices. However, this text does not provide clear evidence that Paul was negating the importance of the Jewish Sabbath and holidays.

And a quick note about Galatians 4:10–11. The common viewpoint that Paul was diminishing Shabbat and the holidays stands on weak ground. In its notes on Galatians 4:10–11, the *ESV Study Bible* confidently asserts Paul is again snuffing out Jewish practice, in general, for Christ-followers: "Days and months and seasons and years were all part of the ceremonial laws of the Mosaic covenant. To require Christians to follow such OT laws is to forfeit the gospel of justification by faith alone."[81]

The *ESV Study Bible's* commentary is comparable to the pastor's perspective I referred to earlier. In other words, an emphasis on Torah observance/Mosaic covenant is incompatible with "the gospel of justification by faith alone." But here's the thing. Galatians 4:10–11 does not have the Torah/Mosaic covenant in view.

The days, months, seasons, and years referenced were not Jewish/Torah/Mosaic days, months, seasons, and years. Instead, the context strongly suggests Paul referred to dates and seasons associated with Gentile/pagan observances. The verses preceding Galatians 4:10–11 point convincingly in this direction:

> Formerly, when you did not know God, you were enslaved to those that by nature are not gods. But now that you have come to know God, or rather to be known by God, how can you turn back again to the weak and worthless elementary principles of the world, whose slaves you want to be once more? You observe days and months and seasons and years! I am afraid I may have labored over you in vain. (Gal 4:8–11)

The language in verses 8–9 is a dead giveaway that Paul was speaking to Gentiles about their former pagan way of life. It is highly improbable that a Jew like Paul would use such language to refer to Jewish Torah observances that God ordained *in the Bible*. In other words, as a Jew, Paul would not refer to times and seasons that God established in the Torah as "weak and worthless elementary principles." That's the way Jews spoke about pagan things. It's not the way Jews spoke about Jewish/biblical things. Additionally, in verse 10, if Paul were discouraging a "turning back" to a Jewish calendar, it is hard to imagine that he would not include explicit Jewish communal terms such as "weeks" and "Sabbaths" in his list of what not to become enslaved to.[82] Again, it's a return to pagan practices, not Jewish ones, that Paul discouraged here.

While Colossians 2 and Galatians 4 are frequently marshaled to suggest Paul diminished the importance of the Sabbath and Jewish holidays in his letters, there are much more probable ways to understand these texts that do not pit the apostle against fundamental Jewish observances.

DID PAUL PRESENT CHRIST-FOLLOWERS AS A REPLACEMENT FOR THE JERUSALEM TEMPLE?

Earlier, I made a case that the Jerusalem Temple was a refuge for Paul. And I said, like the Torah, the Jerusalem Temple was a little something against the wind for the Weird Apostle. As you read, I'm sure some of you wondered how Paul could have had such a high view of the temple when he wrote in his letters that the ekklesia *replaced* the temple. If that crossed your mind, you are normal. That's the way Paul is typically understood.

Reflecting the mainstream Christian viewpoint regarding Paul, the temple, and the ekklesia, the popular Christian organization the Bible Project says the following:

The New Testament writers continue to use temple language, but they are no longer concerned with a building. When they write about the temple, they are talking about the people of God. . . . In the ancient world, people traveled from far and wide to encounter God at the temple in Jerusalem. Now, the people of God are the temple and take God's presence to the world. . . . Do we need to rebuild that ancient building on the spot where it once stood in order to meet with God? Nope. He is calling you . . . to function as a little temple today, wherever you are.[83]

There is no question that Paul likened the ekklesia to the Jerusalem Temple. He did that in multiple places. One example is 1 Corinthians 3:16–17: "Do you not know that you are God's temple and that God's Spirit dwells in you? If anyone destroys God's temple, God will destroy him. For God's temple is holy, and you are that temple."

Paul saw lots of parallels between the Jerusalem Temple and the ekklesia. In his view, both housed the presence of God, and both needed to maintain the highest levels of sanctity. But the fact that Paul used temple language to describe the community of Christ-followers does not mean he was asserting that the temple had been replaced. Pamela Eisenbaum makes this point with clarity and precision:

Paul's comments are often interpreted to mean that the community is the functional equivalent of the Jerusalem temple, and, in many ways, that is exactly right. If the primary function of the temple is to mediate the divine presence, then any assembly of worshippers functions similarly. Unfortunately, most Christian interpreters move beyond perceiving an analogical equivalence between the temple and community of Christ-believers to interpreting Paul as asserting that the church has superseded the temple and the entire cultic enterprise.[84]

As a Jew who loved the temple, Paul naturally saw parallels between the physical temple building, which housed God's presence, and the spiritual assembly of Christ-followers, which did the same. But Paul's use of temple parallels and metaphors in his letters does not imply that he saw no further use for the temple. His actions in Acts communicate that the Weird Apostle consistently demonstrated affection and a strong commitment to *ha makom* ("the place").

It's important to note that roughly two-thirds of the Torah's commandments are related to the temple. Thus, if Paul was dismissing the relevance of the temple, then he was essentially dismissing the relevance of the Torah. But as we have demonstrated, it is doubtful Paul had a dismissive view of the Torah and the temple. He held both near and dear to his heart. They were, to him, like home.

LANDING PAUL'S WHAT

Let's pull together where we are thus far regarding Paul's what before we discuss the apostle's why.

The book of Acts looks pretty committed and intentional about presenting Paul as a Torah-faithful Jew and as a follower of Jesus. His what in Acts is consistent: Paul kept the Torah.

In Paul's letters, he was not primarily addressing *his* what. He is addressing the what for his Gentile, non-Jewish audience. At times, it can sound like Paul was denigrating Torah observance in general and various commandments about circumcision, the Sabbath, Jewish holidays, and the temple in particular. But that's not what he was actually doing.

Paul's so-called Torah-negative statements spoke to specific circumstances. Namely, Paul was countering viewpoints that insisted Gentiles must convert and become legally Jewish (as represented by circumcision for adult males) and fully observe the Torah to be justified before God. Paul opposed that viewpoint strongly.

The apostle's good-news message to Gentiles was based firmly on the idea that they can be redeemed and made right with God through Christ alone. Full Torah observance, symbolized by circumcision, is a covenant calling for Jews like Paul, not for Gentiles.

Paul's what, consistently as a follower of Jesus, was that he kept the Torah as a way of life.

PAUL'S DEBATED WHY—AND THE CONSEQUENCES OF HOW THIS QUESTION IS ANSWERED

So if Paul's what as a follower of Jesus was shaped by observing the Torah, how about his why?

- Why did the Torah continue serving as a refuge for him— so he could testify in Acts 28:17 that he had done nothing against the Torah/Judaism-informed customs of his Jewish people?
- Why, as Acts 20:16 records, did the apostle hurry past Ephesus to be in Jerusalem for Shavuot/Pentecost?
- Why did Paul say in Romans 3:1–2 that there is much value in circumcision?

It's all good at this point if you think, "I don't care why Paul lived the way he lived. What matters is what he did and how he lived. And already, you are helping me see that his what was quite different, and certainly stranger, then I realized."

Well, good, then we are making some progress! But bear with me. The why behind Paul's weird lifestyle is a big deal. Paul's why will not only help us understand him and his letters better, but it can also significantly affect how things proceed in the relationship between Christians and Jews. I learned this firsthand through an uncomfortable encounter not long ago.

CHAPTER 7

Paul's Weird Lifestyle, Part 2

The apostle's unchanging colors

DECEPTIVE DRESS-UP AND AN AWKWARD PHONE CALL

It was a Sunday afternoon when I received an unexpected phone call from Jacob.[85]

"Hey, man, I've got a weird situation I want to ask you about." The way Jacob framed it, I knew this would not be an easy or short conversation. But I had no idea what was coming.

Jacob and I had been teammates in a local Atlanta synagogue softball league for the past three years—and he knew I was involved in Jewish-Christian education and relations. Thus, I was a logical person for him to call as he tried to make sense of a situation in the Atlanta Jewish community. For a year, a Christian man had been disguising himself as an Orthodox Jew and functioning as part of a local synagogue. Over time, the man became more comfortable and began subtly evangelizing.

It didn't take long for synagogue members to begin chatting about this. They swiftly asked the man to leave the congregation, but not before he had already created a sense of betrayal, confusion, and confirmation for some in the Jewish community. Confirmation in the sense that once again Christians were using dishonorable tactics to "convert" Jews.

On the other side of the phone, I heard the confusion in Jacob's voice. "What would motivate someone to do that? Can you explain this?" he asked. "Why did this guy dress and act like us when that's not who he is? Was this guy even Jewish? Does Christianity justify or encourage such behavior?"

This was a difficult conversation. I shared with Jacob that most Christians would abhor such deceptive behavior. That helped him—a little. But Jacob and others in the Atlanta Jewish community felt deceived and violated. Sadly, this was not the first time Christian subterfuge has been unmasked in the Jewish community, in Atlanta and many other places. This was an extreme case carried out by a lone man acting independently. However, it was categorically not out of the ordinary. I have personally observed other well-known, mainstream Christian organizations dressing up as religious Jews as a tactic to evangelize religious Jews. That is to say they act as if they are Torah-observant Orthodox Jews with the hopes that their disguises will entice such Jews to believe in Jesus.

So here's the question: Does the why behind Paul's what justify such modern Christian missionary tactics? In other words, did Paul keep the Torah (his what) for the purpose of evangelizing Jews (his why)?

THE MAINSTREAM VIEW: A TORAH-FLEXIBLE PAUL

Most commentators agree Paul's motive for observing the Torah as a follower of Jesus was to be a more effective evangelist to his Jewish brothers and sisters. Paul's relationship with the Torah was flexible and adaptable—his what depended on his company. If he was with Gentiles, he did not observe the Torah. If he was with Jews, he did.

According to this understanding of Paul, the gospel justified such inconsistency. The principal text for supporting the prevailing viewpoint of a Torah-malleable Paul is 1 Corinthians 9:19–23:

> For though I am free from all, I have made myself a servant to all, that I might win more of them. To the Jews I became as a Jew, in order to win Jews. To those under the law I became as one under the law (though not being myself under the law) that I might win those under the law. To those outside the law I became as one outside the law (not being outside the law of God but under the law of Christ) that I might win those outside the law. To the weak I became weak, that I might win the weak. I have become all things to all people, that by all means I might save some. I do it all for the sake of the gospel, that I may share with them in its blessings.

The highly influential Christian pastor and theologian John MacArthur offers standard commentary on this text: "Paul would be as culturally and socially Jewish as necessary when witnessing to Jews. He was not bound to ceremonies and traditions of Judaism. All legal restraints had been removed."[86]

MacArthur and many other commentators draw this conclusion from 1 Corinthians 9:19–23[87] primarily because they understand Paul to be explaining his *behavioral* flexibility in relation to the Torah. According to this viewpoint, Paul acted like Jews when among Jews. He acted "under the law" to win those under the law—though he noted he was not under the law himself. He acted as one "outside the law" (presumably with reference to Gentiles) among those outside the law. And to the weak, he acted weak. Then, in verse 23, Paul delivered a big why for what he did: "For the sake of the gospel."

Again, most Christians would decry the extreme tactics employed by the Atlanta Christian man toward the Jewish community in the earlier story. However, the standard reading of 1 Corinthians 9:19–23 justifies missionary maneuvers involving significant behavioral elasticity.

But a growing chorus of biblical scholars are pushing back on this standard reading—and how we define Paul's why. These scholars are asking some good, essential questions:

- Is Paul's flexibility in 1 Corinthians 9:19–23 best described as behavioral or rhetorical?
- Doesn't a Paul who acted Jewish over here and Gentile over there amount to a trickster?
- If Paul kept kosher with Jews and ate non-kosher with Gentiles, wouldn't such shifty activity have been discovered and criticized?

Personally, I agree that a Paul whose Torah observance (his what) was driven by purely evangelistic goals (his why) paints an unflattering picture of the apostle as a chameleon who changed colors based on his environment.

No matter how greatly Paul valued the gospel, can the apostle's actions be defended if he presented himself as something he was not as a method of persuasion?

In response to the traditional portrait of Paul as a character who only kept the Torah when it was expedient to do so, a man and an unlikely movement have emerged that provide a convincing counternarrative to the chameleon Paul.

NANOS AND THE RISE OF PAUL WITHIN JUDAISM

Dr. Mark Nanos. Before reading this book, I'm guessing you had not heard of him. Nanos is a game changer you need to know.

For a long time, Nanos[88] was like a talented musician who should have been performing in venues seating thousands but was only playing gigs in local joints for ten to twenty people who barely paid attention. Nanos and his perspective within Pauline studies should have a much larger stage by now. But that is changing. The "music" he and other scholars like him produce is getting more airtime.

Nanos is a Jewish historian who specializes in studying Paul within Judaism. He has led the charge in an expanding movement of Jewish scholars who have dedicated their academic pursuits to reframing Jesus, Paul, and the entire New Testament in its Jewish and inter-Judaism context. This academic emphasis on the Jewishness of the New Testament is picking up steam—for example, *The Jewish Annotated New Testament*, edited by Amy-Jill Levine and Marc Zvi Brettler, is now in its second edition.[89] In 2015, Nanos and Magnus Zetterholm served as general editors for the book *Paul within Judaism*,[90] a collection of cutting-edge essays that challenge traditional assumptions about Paul. Not only do these works represent significant developments in restoring Paul to his first-century context, but they also make Paul weird again.

Off in the distance, I can hear the voice of my grandfather, Johnny. "The Jewishness of Jesus? How could that be," I'm sure he would say. "And the Jewishness of Paul? Impossible."

Based on the vile persecution he received from Christians for being a Jew, in his wildest dreams Johnny never could have conceived of a day when Jews would seek to reclaim Jesus and Paul as characters within Judaism. But it's happening—slowly but surely.

And it would blow Johnny's mind that some scholars who identify as Christians[91] are part of this movement as well.

BACK TO THE CHAMELEON PAUL . . . AND WAS PAUL A LIAR FOR THE GOSPEL?

Nanos argues that 1 Corinthians 9:19–23 has been widely misunderstood, with significant implications for how Paul's lifestyle is interpreted. Nanos sees major problems with the standard Christian view of this text, which he describes:

> In order to win different groups, Paul is represented engaging in conduct that can be variously described as "mimicking," "imitating," "deceiving," "tricking," or "aping," the conduct of the other in Torah-defined terms, e.g., observing Torah among Jews and idol-related activity among non-Jews, but without sharing the others' propositional convictions in either case.[92]

For Nanos, such a way of understanding Paul's what raises a major moral concern. Nanos is right. The traditional viewpoint makes Paul into a cunning deceiver who acted Jewish with Jews and Gentile-ish among Gentiles. And this shifty behavior was justified, according to the traditional Christian viewpoint, "for the sake of the gospel."

But Nanos represents a minority of scholars who have countered the chameleon version of Paul in favor of an apostle whose what was consistent. In other words, Nanos posits that the adaptability described in 1 Corinthians 9:19–23 is about Paul's *rhetoric*, not his lifestyle:

Instead of interpreting his explanation of his strategy in terms of adapting [to] the lifestyle of others, Paul is describing his argumentative strategy. He seeks to argue for the propositional truth of the gospel beginning from the premises of each kind of person and group among which he finds himself. This approach represents "rhetorical adaptability," that is, varying one's speech to different audiences by reasoning from their premises. The implications for behavior are completely different.[93]

According to Nanos, Paul's evangelistic strategy involved adapting his rhetoric but not his behavior or lifestyle. In this way, Paul could speak to Jews and non-Jews while still being a Torah-faithful (and morally consistent) Jew within Judaism. This viewpoint is not only a sound and probable exegesis of 1 Corinthians 9:19–23, but it also frees Paul of the charges of being dishonest, cunning, and inconsistent.

Paul was not a trickster. And he wasn't a chameleon. He was a Jewish man who was persuaded that the Messianic Era had dawned because of the death and resurrection of Jesus the Messiah. He was also firmly committed to what he believed was a divinely ordained vocation to deliver this good-news message to diverse communities across the Roman empire. Such a mission required an immense capacity to adapt one's rhetoric, demeanor, and methods of persuasion based on the audience at hand. But it did not require Paul to slyly modify his what to make himself blend in with his audience.

Recently, my wife and I experienced Jewish adaptability that reminded me of Paul in an unexpected place.

JEWISH ADAPTABILITY IN . . . CABO SAN LUCAS

There are Jews in Mexico. Yes, I know Mexico is not the first place that comes to mind when you think of Jewish communities around the world.

But there are Jews all over Central and South America. And wherever there is an identifiable Jewish presence in these areas (or anywhere else in the world), you will likely find a Jewish organization called Chabad.[94]

Chabad is headquartered in the Crown Heights section of Brooklyn, New York. I respect Chabad for several reasons. One is that nothing will stop Chabad from helping Jews to have an opportunity to connect with Judaism—no matter where Jews are found. And one of Chabad's key ingredients is its ability to adapt itself to reach incredibly diverse Jewish audiences worldwide.

But here's what's so impressive. No matter where Chabad goes, their emissaries, called *shluchim*, maintain the highest standards of Torah observance. That means if they are in a remote area, which they often are, Chabad shluchim figure out a way to ship in kosher items if such food is unavailable locally.

Chabad shluchim are true modern-day masters of Jewish adaptability. In fact, my wife and I saw this firsthand when we visited a Chabad in Cabo San Lucas, on the southern tip of Mexico's Baha California peninsula.

The Cabo Chabad *shliach* (emissary), Rabbi Benny, was amazing. He spoke Spanish, English, and Hebrew and was comfortable adjusting his language to the diverse audiences who came through his synagogue door.

The synagogue itself included architectural features with local flare. But make no mistake—though Rabbi Benny was far from Chabad's headquarters in Brooklyn, he and his family lived completely faithful to the Torah.

Rabbi Benny, and Chabad shluchim around the world, do this every day. They adapt their rhetoric and their approach based on their local audience. Their audiences include religious Jews, non-religious Jews, and frequently Christians and various spiritual seekers. Nevertheless, Chabad shluchim remain as loyal to the Torah as their Jewish brothers and sisters in Jerusalem and Crown Heights.

Not all that different than what one might experience in modern times with Chabad, Paul's what as a Torah-observant Jew remained a consistent anchor and source of direction, wherever the winds took him. In other words, Paul's what, as a shliach for Jesus, remained consistent on his missionary journeys.

Famously, Acts 17 describes Paul in conversation with elite philosophers at the Areopagus in Athens. Paul's words in that account demonstrate significant rhetorical adaptability. He modified his message and approach to accommodate his audience. But should we also suspect that Paul "became one as outside the law" by offering worship to the gods of these philosophers? Or should we assume Paul modified his behavior to engage in the sexual activity that defined daily life for Athens locals? There is no evidence that Paul participated in any of those activities. That's because, like Rabbi Benny, Paul lived a consistently Torah-observant life because he had an internal why that anchored him and allowed him to stay faithful to his covenant calling as a Jew.

So, what is the why that drives Jews like Rabbi Benny and Paul to maintain such strong allegiance to the Torah—even in the face of such contrary wind?

BRINGING HOME PAUL'S WHY AT FROM THE EARTH

Paul kept the Torah as a follower of Jesus because it never crossed his mind to do otherwise. Now, of course, we'll go deeper than that. But, honestly, the simplicity of such a statement might be how Paul would define his why. Imagine us, again, back at our meeting at From the Earth:

From the Earth often features local bands on Thursday evenings. And I realize my foot is tapping along with the beat of "Free Fallin'" that is being performed inside the restaurant by tonight's Tom Petty cover band. It's a good thing we are seated outside. This conversation is too important to get distracted. And Tom Petty music can certainly have that effect on me. Tuning out the music, I dial in my full attention.

"Paul, I think you've been misrepresented as someone who stopped keeping the Torah once you became a follower of Jesus," I say. "Now myself, and a growing minority of Christians, Jews, and others, are trying to change that part of how your story is told. We think you lived a Torah-faithful life as a follower of Jesus. But here's my question: What was your why? Why did you continue keeping the Torah as a follower of Jesus?"

"Ryan, there must be a question behind your question," Paul says. "Why wouldn't I keep the Torah? I'm a Jew. And for Jews, faithfulness to God is defined by the commandments of the Torah. What is there to discuss here?"

"I think you've gathered, Paul, that for the past two thousand years the overwhelming perception is that once you became a follower of Jesus, you no longer saw yourself as obligated to the Torah—essentially, you left Judaism. Most people will say you continued to live as a Jew . . . but you didn't keep the Torah or identify with Judaism anymore. Most will acknowledge that you kept some Torah when you were evangelizing Jews. Other than that, most think you were liberated from the Torah."

"Well, if that's how I'm perceived, you and your little band of people who agree with you have a lot of work to do. I'll say this for now. My allegiance to Jesus and my assignment to spread the message about him to Gentiles did not change anything regarding my covenant obligations. This thing about being Jewish and not keeping the Torah makes no sense. It's gibberish. Plenty of Jews don't keep the Torah—both then and now. But Jews who want to live lives that show honor and love for God . . . those Jews keep the Torah. Why would Jesus change that? Jesus himself kept the Torah. The Torah is God's gift to Israel and, in many ways, to the entire world.

"As for why I keep it—just for the record," he continues, "it's because God made an agreement with us, the Jewish people. It's like I wrote in my letter to Rome—to the Jews belong the adoption, the glory, the covenants, the giving of the Torah, the temple service, and the promises. And from us, God sent the patriarchs and the Messiah. So why would I keep the Torah? Because, as a Jew, it is my privilege and obligation to do so. It's how I show my love for God. That, Ryan, is why."

Whether it's Rabbi Benny or Paul, the math for Jews is simple: A fundamental component to a life of faithfulness to God is that you keep the Torah.

To be clear, the Torah is not literally everything for Jews when it comes to faithfulness. For Jews like Paul, faithfulness to God also fundamentally included allegiance to Jesus as the Messiah. For Jews like Rabbi Benny, faithfulness to God includes fidelity to Jewish traditions that have developed over the past two thousand years, especially those found within the Chasidic realm. Other Jews have various components in their faithfulness equation. Judaism is not, and never has been, monolithic.

But for all Jews seeking to honor God within the broad orbit of Judaism, the Torah is a grounding force that defines holiness, distinguishes them from other groups, and keeps them within the boundaries of the covenant God established with them as a nation. As it says *within* the Torah in Leviticus 20:22–24:

> You shall therefore keep all my statutes and all my rules and do them, that the land where I am bringing you to live may not vomit you out. And you shall not walk in the customs of the nation that I am driving out before you, for they did all these things, and therefore I detested them. But I have said to you, "You shall inherit their land, and I will give it to you to possess, a land flowing with milk and honey." I am the Lord your God, who has separated you from the peoples.

Thus, for religious Jews, the Torah is much more than a little something against the wind. It is a massive fortress of protection and guidance from which Jews can fulfill their calling to be a light to the nations.

That is why Paul kept the Torah. And it's why Jews of all kinds continue keeping it to this day.

THE ART IS WRONG

Every single piece of artwork that depicts the Apostle Paul is wrong.

Yes, I sound like an annoying politician or a dogmatic podcaster. And, yes, please do contact me if you know of any exceptions.

Actually, there is at least one exception: The magnificent, spectacular, amazing piece of art depicting the Apostle Paul with a subtle Jewish vibe (à la the Jerusalem background) that you can find . . . on the cover of *this* book.

Yes, that statement about the book cover was over the top because, as you might have guessed, my wife is the artist behind the cover design.

But dialing it down and in, here's the point: Paul has been (mis) framed.

And the muddled picture we have of Paul's lifestyle is not limited to art. Art is a medium to communicate ideas. And the prevailing views about Paul's what and why have been profoundly distorted in books, commentaries, sermons, and stories.

As a follower of Jesus, Paul was not only a Jew. The Weird Apostle was a Jew who consistently kept the Torah within Judaism as an apostle to the nations. And that what was driven by a clear why.

Paul kept the Torah as a follower of Jesus *because* there was no question in his mind that the Jewish people continued having a covenant role and calling in this world. The Torah was the constitution God gave to the Jews. Abandoning it, for Paul and other Jews across the broad landscape of Judaism, is tantamount to abandoning God.

That's a weird way of thinking about Paul's lifestyle. But evidence from the book of Acts and his letters points strongly in that direction: "To them [Jews/Israelites] belong the adoption, the glory, the covenants, the giving of the law, the worship, and the promises . . . I had done nothing against our people or the customs of our fathers" (Rom 9:4; Acts 28:17).

The familiar Paul found in most books, commentaries, sermons, and artwork could not have said those words. Those words were made by someone who upholds the ongoing validity of the Torah and Judaism for himself and his fellow Jews. But, in fact, those words *were* Paul's in Romans 9:4 and Acts 28:17.

It's time for our books, commentaries, sermons, and artwork to regain alignment with the weird lifestyle of the Weird Apostle. The Torah was a shelter for Paul. It was something against the wind for him. It was home. And it was an anchor that guided his behavior before and after he became a follower of Jesus and an apostle to the Gentiles.

For most people, that's a massive paradigm shift with many implications. But just as the standard Torah-free view of Paul has had profound ramifications for Christians and Jews in the past, changes in how we view Paul's lifestyle can have a profoundly positive effect as we build the future.

GAME-CHANGING ACTION

Okay, so what now? How can we change the framing of Paul's lifestyle? And why does this matter?

Let's start with Christians.

For Christians, Paul is a massive deal. The thirteen New Testament letters bearing his name have tremendous weight and value in shaping Christian thought and life. But, typically, Paul is not presented as a character who encouraged Christians to see the Torah as a primary source of wisdom and instruction. And learning the Torah as a fundamental part of Christian discipleship? That is a bizarre, almost unimaginable concept.

But what if that's what Paul intended? Imagine Paul saying something like this in a preface to a modern book on Christian spiritual growth: "A key part of learning about Jesus is learning the Bible that he followed. Thus, remember to give plenty of attention to learning the Torah. The Torah is an indispensable component of living a righteous life for all followers of Jesus." This statement would not get your book endorsed by most Christian leaders, but it's consistent with the letters written by the Weird Apostle.

In Paul's second letter to Timothy, he wrote, "All Scripture is breathed out by God and profitable for teaching, for reproof, for correction, and for training in righteousness, that the man of God may be complete, equipped for every good work" (2 Tim 3:16–17).

"All Scripture," when Paul wrote these words, referred to the Torah and, by extension, to the entire Old Testament. For Paul, equipping Christians for every good work included learning the Torah.

It's weird to consider that Paul directly advised Gentile Christ-followers that the Torah was "profitable . . . for training in righteousness." What if more Christians embraced a portrait of the apostle's lifestyle, including Paul's love for the Torah and Judaism? The result would include Christians seeing more value and the wisdom that can be gained in the first two-thirds of their Bibles. While

Paul adamantly opposed turning Gentiles into Jews, he nonetheless continued upholding the ongoing validity of the Torah and Judaism for *everyone*.

While I wrote this chapter, a friend reminded me that Romans 15:4 contains another component of Paul's why: "For whatever was written in former days was written for our instruction, that through endurance and through the encouragement of the Scriptures we might have hope."

The "whatever" written in "former days" for "our instruction" is the Torah and the entire Old Testament. My friend scribbled this on a tattered piece of paper taped to a window: "For everything that was written in the past was meant to teach us." That's beautiful.

What would happen if more Christians saw the *current* teaching value of what was "written in the past"? According to Paul, there is a significant spiritual payoff. As he said, that "written in former days" is fuel for "endurance" . . . and "the encouragement of the Scriptures" leads to "hope" (Romans 15:4).

This alone would be a game changer for Christians. But there's more.

With huge positive implications, more Christians viewing the Torah as a source of instruction and encouragement would improve relationships between Christians and Jews because they would have a shared interest in learning from a source both see as life-giving.

Christians would no longer see the Torah as outdated or replaced by Christ. They would see that Christ and Paul upheld these things and that they should also. I believe this would create a tangible sense in which Christians view the Torah and Judaism as anchors for their faith, not only in the past but in the present. It is encouraging to note that some modern-day Christians are already moving in this direction. And while these Christians don't seek to be Jews, they aim to understand the validity of the Torah for their lives as disciples of Christ.[95]

Strangely, for a growing number of modern Christians, the Torah is becoming a little something against the wind for them also. It provides an additional layer to their foundation that they sensed was not only lacking but essential. As my friend Rabbi Jason Sobel says, some Christians are no longer settling for half of an inheritance. And this is happening largely because of a new (and weird) way of seeing Paul.

As Christians gain momentum in seeing Paul's lifestyle as a Torah-observant Jew, this view will also increasingly disarm those who have used Paul's writings as weapons to denigrate the Torah, Jews, and Judaism. As Matthew Novenson says, "Most Protestant theologies of Paul require a foe for the apostle to vanquish, and most have made Judaism play the part of that foe."[96] Historically, Paul has been used more than any other biblical source not only to make Jews and Judaism a foe, but to demonize both.

But imagine if the tables turned and the dominant view of Paul became that he was a Torah-loving, Judaism-keeping, loyal Jew who passionately followed Jesus? Rather than reacting numbly to citations of Paul used to disparage Jews and Judaism, Christians would push back against such harmful statements. This would be a welcome and massive step forward in repairing the bridge between Christians and Jews—their differences notwithstanding.

For Jews, the prevailing picture of Paul's lifestyle has been framed by what they have observed from Christian discourse on the apostle. Thus, being that Christians have historically presented Paul outside of Judaism at best and harshly against it at worst, the Jewish community understandably views him with great suspicion.

But what if a new image emerged, redrawing the Apostle Paul as someone who aimed to spread the principles of Torah and Judaism to the world *because* of his convictions about Jesus? That is a very weird and understandably uncomfortable thought for most Jews. But this is the Paul of history. And it's a Paul whose image can be rehabilitated in the Jewish community.

Significantly, in the past fifty years, the Jewish world has made tremendous gains in refurbishing the Jewishness of Jesus.

Jesus as the Jewish Messiah? No.

Jesus as a Jew who lived a faithful Jewish life? Many Jews have been saying yes for several generations. And this has undoubtedly assisted in narrowing the deep divide between Christians and Jews.

But Paul is a different story. And I believe Paul remains the largest wall to scale in this relationship. Historically, the Jewish community has viewed Paul as a traitor who abandoned the Torah, Judaism, and his people. And this viewpoint remains widespread. More than a few Jews have said, "Jesus, yes! Paul, never!"

Saint Paul, for Jews, is considered anything but saintly. He is the real villain in the Christian story who started a new religion, Christianity, to replace Judaism, which he determined was empty and devoid of spiritual life. This view of Paul remains deeply entrenched in the Jewish community.

However, just like some Christians are starting to shift the Paul narrative, some Jews—like Nanos and others—are also. But we need more Jews to reclaim Paul as the Torah-faithful, Judaism-loving Jew he was. Such a narrative shift can happen without Jews agreeing with Paul about the identity of Jesus. It's possible for the Jewish community to respect Paul without agreeing with him. Imagine if we toppled some of these barriers so Paul could be appreciated for exporting the values of Judaism worldwide! Yes, he did so centered upon the idea that Jesus is the Messiah. But that doesn't change the fact that he represented a Jewish cause that aimed to bring Torah values and the worship of Israel's God to all of humanity. No Jew other than Jesus has been so instrumental in spreading intrinsic Jewish principles throughout the earth. Not even close.

While Jews will understandably maintain reluctance and distance regarding Paul's commitment to Jesus, we can nonetheless embrace him as a Jew who stood with his people. Such a game-changing perspective would also help Jews feel more kinship with Christians. Currently, such kinship is not so easy to create, so long as the anti-Torah, anti-Judaism, and even anti-Semitic portrait of Paul remains the dominant image Jews have about Paul. But if that script is flipped, we can begin seeing

Paul as a link between Christians and Jews. Jews would still see Paul as a Christ-follower, but he would also be seen as one of their own. And for Jews to know one of their guys is on the inside of Christianity, it may just help to create meaningful engagement.

Paul loved Jesus, and he was persuaded everyone else should too. However, that conviction did not negate his lifelong commitment to the Torah and Judaism. The Torah was Paul's anchor. It was his home and shelter, again and again.

CHAPTER 8

Paul's Weird Rule, Part 1

A call for unity, not uniformity

ONE

Bono. His voice inspired a generation.

Gosh, I love U2. What a blend of passion, creativity, rhythm, and Bono's powerful presence as the lead singer. And yes, I am listening to them as I write this.

Picking a favorite U2 song is tough. There's "With or Without You," "Where the Streets Have No Name." They have so many great numbers.

But their song "One" stands at the top of my list. "One" is mostly about the pain of a failed relationship. But it's the end of the song that moves me. Bono goes universal with the final lyrics, talking about how we have one life to live, thus we should seek unity in our relationships despite our differences. Give the song a listen. It's a stirring finale.

Strangely, that idea—that we are united, yet still different— parallels Paul's weird rule.

PAUL'S (NOT SO) FAMOUS RULE

I have observed an interesting phenomenon over the past twenty-five years of studying Paul. Outside of academia, few people who care about Paul have any idea that he has a rule.

When I mention "Paul's rule," I imagine many of you are doing a mental index. Especially for Christian readers, questions may be swirling. *Paul's rule? Wait, did he actually have a rule? Does this have something to do with the Holy Spirit? It seems like I saw something, somewhere, where Paul talked about a rule. Oh, yes, Paul's rule was that we are saved by faith, not by works. Right?*

Okay, you can stop flipping brain files. Let me put you at ease. Whether you are Jewish or Christian or neither, you are normal if you are hazy or entirely in the dark regarding this "Paul's rule" thing.

But here is *the thing*: If Paul had a rule for all his Christ-following communities—and if he used unique language by introducing it as "my rule"—wouldn't that be a big deal? Of course. Paul is one of the most influential humans in history and the most prolific writer in the New Testament. So it's a big deal if he had a unique, distinct rule.

Well, Paul indeed had such a rule. It's weird that something so big is so small in how Paul is typically visualized and understood. And Paul's rule was weird—weird, that is, to us. But his rule was a central feature of his good-news message.

Paul's rule, outlined in 1 Corinthians 7:17–20, protected a revolutionary component of his world-changing gospel. Just like the U2 song, even though the followers of Jesus are one, they are not the same.

HAVE YOU READ GALATIANS?

Whenever I suggest that, in Paul's mind, Jews and Gentiles have *different* responsibilities and expressions within the ekklesia (church), I typically hear this defense: "Have you read Galatians?"

You and I could have dinner at one of Atlanta's finest restaurants if I had a dollar for every time someone quickly redirected the conversation to Galatians when I bring up Paul's rule in 1 Corinthians 7 and his commitment to *distinction* among Christ-followers.

So, let's make a quick visit over to Galatians.

It's a natural Christian reflex to spray something from Galatians to snuff out the odor of discrimination and to eliminate the scent of difference *among Christ-followers*. And one verse serves as the ultimate cleanser: "There is neither Jew nor Greek, there is neither slave nor free, there is no male and female, for you are all one in Christ Jesus" (Gal 3:28).

In Christ Jesus, there are no Jews and no Greeks. You are all one in Christ Jesus. That sounds pretty straightforward. There's not much debate in Christian commentaries about Paul's meaning in this verse.

In his commentary on Galatians, the highly esteemed New Testament scholar James Dunn says, "'Neither Jew nor Greek' means oneness of Jew and Gentile in faith, without the law's interposing between them to mark them off as distinct from each other."[97] The *ESV Study Bible* says much of the same in its comments on Galatians 3:28: "The fact that the Mosaic law has been left behind in the old age means that, in the new creation, the distinction between Jew and Gentile is broken down."[98]

If you consult one Christian commentary on Galatians 3:28, then you have pretty much consulted them all. There is a broad consensus about Paul's meaning in this verse: Jewish and Gentile identities no longer carry any significant value among the followers of Jesus. In Christ, all such distinctions have been eliminated.

On the surface and in isolation, it's not hard to draw this conclusion. But if we dig deeper and are willing to question what is familiar, it becomes apparent that there are some problems with this largely uncontested interpretation of Galatians 3:28.

I agree with the general Christian consensus that Galatians 3:28 is a strong call for unity. But unity and uniformity are two different things. This famous verse does present Paul as a champion of oneness. However, it does *not* support the idea that Paul was eliminating all levels of differentiation within the kingdom of God.

In the text, Paul said there is neither Jew nor Greek. But he also said there is no male and female. If Paul's point was to eliminate all distinctions between Jews and Gentiles, to remain consistent, he would also be saying there are no longer distinctions between genders. Elsewhere, Paul explicitly addressed and differentiated between males and females. So, it's hard to imagine Paul altogether eliminating the categories listed in Galatians 3:28.

So if Paul wasn't erasing the distinction between Jews and Gentiles or males and females, then what was his point? To get there, we need to zoom out from this verse and discuss why Paul wrote his letter to the Galatians in the first place.

THE OCCASION FOR GALATIANS

Paul wrote Galatians in response to what he felt was a harmful, apparently influential idea circulating in the Galatian, Christ-following community. The "influencers" Paul sought to counter advocated for Christ-following Gentiles to become legally Jewish, symbolized by circumcision, if they wanted to become members of equal and righteous standing within the kingdom of God. This made Paul furious.

The apostle to the Gentiles countered vigorously by ensuring the Galatians that if they had *pistis* (faith), they had a right standing with God through the justifying work of Christ alone. Thus, becoming Jewish through circumcision was not only unnecessary, but it also undermined Paul's gospel, which emphasized that their new identity in Christ fully secured their standing before God and within the ekklesia. Two verses before Galatians 3:28, Paul wrote, "For in Christ Jesus you are all sons of God, through faith. For as many of you as were baptized into Christ have put on Christ" (Gal 3:26–27).

In-Christ Gentiles, Paul said, are *all sons of God* through *pistis*. Paul argued that his Gentiles' standing within the family of God was stable and secure because of their new in-Christ identity. That is reaffirmed in Galatians 3:29: "And if you are Christ's, then you are Abraham's offspring, heirs according to promise." Gentiles in Christ are "sons" and part of Abraham's family. According to Paul, equal standing within this family is obtained "through faith" and "in Christ" and, very importantly, not through circumcision.

If the influencers Paul was countering were correct, then Gentiles needed to become Jews to have a justified standing before God and within the ekklesia. But that's not the case, Paul said. Gentiles in Christ do not need to be circumcised and become Jews to be made right with God. And in that sense, Paul said, "There is neither Jew nor Greek."

As my old friend and the excellent Bible teacher Daniel Lancaster notes in his commentary on Galatians, "Jews, Gentiles, men, women, slaves, and free-men have the same access to salvation through the same Messiah, but that does not eliminate our distinct identities and roles."[99] Lancaster's is a rare perspective on this famous verse, but he's on the money. Galatians 3:28 expresses Paul's view regarding equal access to God's salvation. But it does not eliminate the distinct roles of Jews and Gentiles.

And that leads us to Paul's rule.

The Weird Apostle's rule harmonized with his message in Galatians. His rule insisted upon boundaries that did not oppress but instead protected the freedom of diversity and unique identities within the Christ movement.

Now, let's look closely at Paul's rule in all the churches.

SO, WHAT IS PAUL'S RULE?

Again, it's strange how many fans, students, and critics of Paul are unaware that he communicated his rule in plain daylight in his first letter to the Corinthians. So, let's take a look at it. And as you read Paul's rule below, here's a tip: You might find it helpful to mentally substitute the word "Jewish" each time Paul refers to circumcision, and "Gentile" or "non-Jew" every time he refers to "uncircumcised."

> Only let each person lead the life that the Lord has assigned to him and to which God has called him. This is my rule in all the churches. Was anyone at the time of his call already circumcised? Let him not seek to remove the marks of circumcision. Was anyone at the time of his call uncircumcised? Let him not seek circumcision. For neither circumcision counts for anything nor uncircumcision, but keeping the commandments of God. Each one should remain in the condition in which he was called. (1 Cor 7:17–20)

So, there it is. He says it right there in verse 17, "This is my rule in all the churches." Again, that's unique language for Paul, so we should take note. As Christian New Testament scholar Brian Tucker says, "The fact that Paul establishes a rule on this topic indicates that it is not a matter of 'indifference' for him but one of fundamental importance."[100]

But what does Paul mean here? Honestly, it's not clear because, as he often does, Paul jumps around a bit. But in the end, Paul brings home his point, saying, "Each one should remain in the condition in which he was called." In other words, Jews (the circumcised) should remain as Jews, and Gentiles (the uncircumcised) should remain as

Gentiles within the ekklesia. That actually does not seem difficult to understand. But, strangely, many Christian commentators interpret Paul to mean the exact opposite.

N. T. Wright, one of the leading New Testament scholars of this generation, says this about Paul's rule: "Paul does not say, in other words, what some dearly wish he had said, namely, that 'Jews and gentiles should stick to their respective ways of life.'"[101]

With all due respect to Wright, I think he is wrong. One does not have to wish for Paul to say that Jews and Gentiles should stick to their respective ways of life. He says it right in this text. That's what he means in verse 20 when he says Jews and Gentiles should "remain in the condition in which they are called."

Now, verse 19 can—and has—created plenty of confusion. It sounds like Paul is casting off the significance of Jewish and Gentile identities when he states, "For neither circumcision counts for anything nor uncircumcision." That is the familiar way this text is typically presented in commentaries, books, and sermons. But this flattening of social identities is a big misinterpretation that severely distorts the Weird Apostle, his gospel, and his rule.

Like we discussed earlier regarding Galatians 3:28, Paul's point in 1 Corinthians 7 was not to diminish the importance of circumcision (or uncircumcision) in general. Instead, Paul countered a popular idea in the early Christ movement that circumcision (a.k.a. becoming a Jew) was a required step for in-Christ Gentiles to ensure their complete justification before God and within the ekklesia. Circumcision *does* mean something very important for Jews, but it means nothing for Gentiles. Paul's rule served to protect Gentiles from taking this step— which would essentially eliminate Gentile identity within the ekklesia. From this text in 1 Corinthians 7, we can sum up Paul's rule like this: Paul's rule is a call to protect distinct identities within the family of God.[102]

The possibility of in-Christ Gentiles undergoing circumcision to bolster or complete their standing before God, in Paul's mind, diminished the immeasurable value of Christ's atoning death, which for his Gentiles served to transform their identities from sinners to saints. This is the sense in which we need to understand Paul's statement that "neither circumcision counts for anything nor uncircumcision." For Gentiles, circumcision cannot transform them from pagans to holy people. For Paul, only Jesus could do that. As the apostle said succinctly in 2 Corinthians 5:17: "Therefore, if anyone is in Christ, he is a new creation. The old has passed away; behold, the new has come."

Again, it's critical that we not read Paul as an opponent of circumcision. Elsewhere, Paul affirmed circumcision is valuable "much in every way" (Rom 3:1). Paul opposed circumcision for in-Christ Gentiles, but he defended it for Jews. This is what his rule intended to uphold.

But why was Paul so over the top about this? He even got nasty at times toward those advocating circumcision for his Gentiles—which would effectively turn them into Jews: "I wish those who unsettle you would emasculate themselves" (Gal 5:12).

Paul was basically cussing out his opponents here. The Weird Apostle was a handful. Well, regardless of Paul's temperament, a deeply rooted hope undergirded his rule, particularly the part about each person remaining in their calling.

For Paul, Jews and Gentiles had to be visible and unified if the end-times movement he was advancing was the one he read about in his Bible.

PAUL'S FAVORITE PROPHET

Whether you love him or hate him, embrace him or reject him, find him compelling or plain boring—hopefully, those who form an opinion of Paul can agree on these two well-substantiated ideas: He was a sharp guy. And he knew his Bible.

With command and fluidity, Paul incorporated direct quotations and indirect allusions from the Jewish Bible/Old Testament throughout his letters. In Romans alone, Paul included forty-two Scripture quotations.

Why did Paul quote the Bible so much in his letters? Because he was persuaded that the Jesus movement was the beginning realization of the end-times redemption envisioned by the Jewish prophets. Acts 28:20 records Paul speaking of this prophetic realization as "the hope of Israel." And the Jewish, biblical hope of the future redemption presented a consistent portrait of two distinct groups that would be present in that longed-for era: Israel and the nations (a.k.a. Jews and Gentiles).

Famously, the prophet Isaiah even foretold a day when *ha-goyim* (the nations/Gentiles/non-Jews) would flock to Jerusalem to learn God's Torah alongside the Jewish people:

It shall come to pass in the latter days
 that the mountain of the house of the Lord
shall be established as the highest of the mountains,
 and shall be lifted up above the hills;
and all the nations shall flow to it,
 and many peoples shall come, and say:
"Come, let us go up to the mountain of the Lord,
 to the house of the God of Jacob,
that he may teach us his ways
 and that we may walk in his paths."
For out of Zion shall go forth the law,
 and the word of the Lord from Jerusalem. (Isa 2:2–3)

Though Paul did not directly quote the above text in his letters, we can be confident he was well acquainted with it because Isaiah was his go-to prophet. In his letter to the Romans alone, Paul directly quoted Isaiah fifteen times and frequently alluded to him indirectly.

Paul quoted Scripture a lot in his letters. But, clearly, Isaiah was his guy. That makes sense for two big reasons.

1. Isaiah talked a lot about the end-times.
2. Isaiah talked a lot about the nations (Gentiles) worshipping the God of Israel in those end-times.

Isaiah 11:10 is one excerpt from a section of this book that is thick with messianic and end-times significance: "In that day the root of Jesse, who shall stand as a signal for the peoples—of him shall the nations inquire, and his resting place shall be glorious." And as he did regularly, the prophet envisioned the presence of non-Jews worshipping the God of Israel alongside the Jewish people. Thus, it was natural and strategic for Paul to quote Isaiah 11:10 within a string of citations from the Old Testament as he unveiled the global and biblical significance of his gospel.

> For I tell you that Christ became a servant to the circumcised to show God's truthfulness, in order to confirm the promises given to the patriarchs, and in order that the Gentiles might glorify God for his mercy. As it is written,
>
> > "Therefore I will praise you among the Gentiles,
> > and sing to your name."
> > And again it is said,
> > "Rejoice, O Gentiles, with his people."
> > And again,
> > "Praise the Lord, all you Gentiles,
> > and let all the peoples extol him."
> > And again Isaiah says,
> > "The root of Jesse will come,
> > even he who arises to rule the Gentiles;
> > in him will the Gentiles hope."

May the God of hope fill you with all joy and peace in believing, so that by the power of the Holy Spirit you may abound in hope.

I myself am satisfied about you, my brothers, that you your-selves are full of goodness, filled with all knowledge and able to instruct one another. But on some points I have written to you very boldly by way of reminder, because of the grace given me by God to be a minister of Christ Jesus to the Gentiles in the priestly service of the gospel of God, so that the offering of the Gentiles may be acceptable, sanctified by the Holy Spirit. In Christ Jesus, then, I have reason to be proud of my work for God. (Rom 15:8–17)

The importance of this text from Paul's letter to the Romans cannot be overstated. Paul was proud (Rom 15:17) of his work among the Gentiles because he interpreted it as the same work Isaiah and other biblical prophets had anticipated in the end-times.

Simply stated, Paul's emphasis on protecting the boundaries of Jewish and Gentile identities, thus ensuring the presence and pres-ervation of both, was rooted in what he read in the Bible regarding God's kingdom. As Paula Fredriksen says, "Like the biblical prophets whose words he drew on, Paul expected God's kingdom to contain two human populations: Israel and the nations. This meant that gentiles needed to remain gentiles."[103]

Messaging and pressuring Gentiles to become Jews, which Paul's other contemporaries in the Jesus movement were doing, under-mined a fundamental component of the Jewish, prophetic redemption program. To Paul, such a message was far too small. And it was too small for the prophet Isaiah also.

It is too light a thing that you should be my servant
    to raise up the tribes of Jacob

and to bring back the preserved of Israel;

I will make you as a light for the nations,

that my salvation may reach to the end of the earth. (Isa 49:6)

In Acts 13:47, Luke recorded that Paul quoted Isaiah 49:6 in one of his synagogue sermons to explain his emphasis on taking the gospel to Gentiles. To the Weird Apostle, the God of Israel was God not just of the Jews, but of all the nations of the earth. He expressed this with passion in Romans 3:29–30: "Or is God the God of Jews only? Is he not the God of Gentiles also? Yes, of Gentiles also, since God is one—who will justify the circumcised by faith and the uncircumcised through faith."

Being both God of the Jews and God of the Gentiles implies unity and distinction. To show there was one God for all required *all* to maintain their distinctiveness. And to ensure that, Paul established his rule for all the churches. Christian theologian Kendall Soulen sums up this concept eloquently:

> The distinction between Jew and Gentile, being intrinsic to God's work as Consummator of creation, is not erased but realized in a new way in the sphere of the church. The church concerns the Jew as a Jew and the Gentile as a Gentile, not only initially or for the period of a few generations but essentially and at all times.[104]

Let's pause for a moment. I've been around these texts and this topic enough to know that at this point, some people might be getting uncomfortable with what I'm saying. This talk of "distinction" sounds a bit like a call for division and separation between Jews and Gentiles. And I know some minds are going to the book of Ephesians, where Paul called for the *abolishment* of the famous dividing wall between Jews and Gentiles.

So, what's happening here? Does this weird reading of Paul—and this emphasis upon the apostle's rule—build walls or tear them down?

IS PAUL'S DIVIDING WALL UP OR DOWN?

I don't often read something that stops me cold. But that happened not long ago when I read the following statement in an essay by Israeli scholars Ishay Rosen-Zvi and Adi Ophir: "If there is a consistent effort in his [Paul's] letters, it is to erect 'the dividing wall,' and not just to 'break [it] down.' Before the two can become one in Jesus (Eph 2.15), they must first appear as two; they must be radically and systematically differentiated."[105]

Did they really say that? Paul's letters include a consistent effort to *erect* "the dividing wall"? That's crazy. It's not even worth considering. After all, everyone knows Paul said "the dividing wall" between Jews and Gentiles was *broken down.*

Speaking of the implications of Christ's death for the relationship between Jews and Gentiles, Ephesians 2:14–15 says, "For he himself is our peace, who has made us both one and has *broken down* in his flesh *the dividing wall* of hostility by abolishing the law of commandments expressed in ordinances, that he might create in himself one new man in place of the two, so making peace."

We know what the "familiar" Paul meant in these verses: There is no longer any difference between Jews and Gentiles. In Christ, the two previously divided groups have become "one new man . . . in place of the two." And, very importantly, as verse 15 says, "the law of commandments expressed in ordinances" (a.k.a. the Torah) has been abolished.

So, this talk of continued differences and dividing walls somehow being connected to Paul's rule . . . well, it's not just weird. It's bad theology. Christ tore all that stuff down. And Paul made that clear. As scholar John Barclay says, "Paul declares that the ethnic distinctions between Jew and Gentile, which [were] foundational to his 'ancestral traditions,' [have] been dissolved by the incongruous gift of Christ."[106]

In light of all this talk about distinctions and walls, maybe my song reference for this chapter should be Pink Floyd's "The Wall" rather than U2's "One."

Yes, some people might think I am advocating for a version of Paul that leads to walls going back up that were meant to be torn down. Well, we have some things to sort out here. Because, actually, I think Rosen-Zvi and Ophir are correct.

Paul did have a rule that built walls. But these were not restrictive walls. I call these "shalom walls." Paul's walls did not keep people out and they did not lock anyone in. Instead, Paul's shalom walls brought liberty, unity, and peace.

I can hear some of you: "Shalom walls? Really. Are you kidding?"

Let's press into this idea a bit further.

PAUL'S SHALOM WALLS

Yes, that rhymes a little. And I dig that. But that's not why I chose the term "shalom walls" to describe Paul's rule. I devised that term because it captures the peace-producing unity/distinction balance in Paul's rule.

Paul did not build discriminatory walls. Instead, his rule established boundaries that protected the diversity of God's kingdom and allowed Jews and Gentiles to maintain their uniqueness as unified Christ-followers. The Pauline scholar William S. Campbell says:

> This is what I think Paul intends us to hear—not that God cannot see, or does not recognize, diversity in peoples, which seems rather strange, but rather that he refuses to discriminate against (certain) people in a certain category because they differ in some respects from others.[107]

Paul was not trying to create separation or discrimination between Jews and Gentiles. And he was certainly not trying to erect an apartheid-type wall between them. In fact, he was doing the very opposite. Paul's rule was designed to uphold an essential feature of God's kingdom: shalom *between* Israel and the nations.

Authentic shalom does not eliminate differences. It allows different groups to coexist in a peaceful, unified manner. This was the vision of the prophets that Paul read about in the Jewish Scriptures.

Okay, okay, so maybe you are starting to see that Paul's rule served to protect the uniqueness and presence of Jews and Gentiles, Israel and the nations. But what does all this mean practically? What does this look like on the ground? Are there different rules for Jews and for Gentiles?

This is where a lot of people get uncomfortable.

In hundreds of conversations about the implications of Paul's rule through the years, I find it's not difficult to get people to see that Paul's rule in all the churches is intended to protect the distinction and calling of Jews and Gentiles. But, ironically, walls and defenses tend to go up when we drill into the implications of this rule and consider the possibility that Paul's rule included not only protecting diversity but also different expectations for Jews and Gentiles. And before long, typically, someone brings out a big gun to end the battle and blow up this dangerous talk—a three-word Pauline concept that is widely misunderstood and misused: one new man.

ONE NEW MAN: A STRONG BUT MISUSED TERM

Many years ago, at the beginning of my journey to discover Paul's view of ongoing identities within the ekklesia, I heard a presentation from Jeff, a Bible teacher, who appealed to 1 Corinthians 10:32 to explain that Paul had only three categories regarding identities: "Give no offense to Jews or to Greeks or to the church of God."

After the presentation, I asked Jeff for clarification. I don't remember his exact words, but I remember his point: There are Jews. There are Greeks. And there are Christians in the church of God. That's it. Those are Paul's three categories, and you can only be in one of them. Christians who continue to identify as Jews, or as Gentiles, are not following what Paul taught in 1 Corinthians 10:32.

I walked away from that conversation unconvinced Jeff was in touch with Paul's meaning in 1 Corinthians 10:32. I didn't know why, but reflexively, I didn't think that was Paul's point.

My continued studies led me toward a more probable option for understanding 1 Corinthians 10:32. Paul's point here was not to draw firm identity categories. Rather, he promoted respectful dynamics between the various groups interacting with his gospel.

But what I heard from Jeff the Bible teacher was important. He was expressing an unrefined but clear argument for a broader Pauline concept called "third race theology," which suggests that Paul advocated for a new Christian identity that erased the significance of all other identities.

You won't hear many folks using the term "third race" to explain their view of Paul—it sounds colonial and, let's be honest, a bit scary and militant. And "third race" is not a term Paul uses. But third-race thinking is common in Christian theology. A more common term used to advocate for the same idea is "one new man." This has a more hopeful ring to it, and it is an actual biblical term found in Ephesians 2:15:

But now in Christ Jesus you who once were far off have been brought near by the blood of Christ. For he himself is our peace, who has made us both one and has broken down in his flesh the dividing wall of hostility by abolishing the law of commandments expressed in ordinances, that he might create in himself *one new man* in place of the two, so making peace, and might reconcile us both to God in one body through the cross, thereby killing the hostility. (Eph 2:13–16)

The prevailing view of the term "one new man" is that both Jewish and Gentile identities have melted or flattened out in favor of a new conglomerate identity or race characterized as Christian or "the church." In fact, several Bible versions, including the ESV cited here, present a translation of Ephesians 2:15 that makes it difficult to conclude otherwise.

Note in the ESV version of Ephesians 2:15 that the one new man is created "in place of the two." If the ESV translation is correct, this verse provides substantial evidence that a superior Christian identity has indeed replaced Jewish and Gentile identities. But as the South African Christian scholar David Woods notes, this is a product of the translators' theology and not the actual text of Ephesians: "The Bible translators supplied 'in place of' in order to clarify the meaning, but the meaning they assume does not correspond with the evidence. . . . I submit that the phrase 'in place of' in some English translations of Ephesians 2:15 is misleading and best omitted."[108]

I agree with Woods. I do not doubt the ESV Bible translators supplied "in place of" as a helpful addition to smooth out a difficult-to-understand text. Bible translators do this kind of thing regularly. But including the phrase "in place of" perpetuates a theological viewpoint inconsistent with Paul's rule and the broader intent of Paul's letter to the Ephesians.

Paul's rule in 1 Corinthians 7 promotes the maintenance of Jewish and Gentile identities. Thus, interpreting "one new man" as the elimination of Jewish and Gentile identities in favor of a new Christian identity is not only an improbable interpretation, but it also undermines the magnitude of the reconciliation and unity Paul believed the ekklesia represented.

Paul's emphasis in Ephesians 2 and the entire letter was that the dividing wall and hostility between Jews and Gentiles had been removed.

Before Christ, as I've noted earlier, Jews categorized Gentiles as pagan sinners and Gentiles categorized Jews as atheists. The boundaries and status quo were clear: Jews and Gentiles worshipped different gods and oriented themselves according to entirely different worldviews.

Paul's argument in Ephesians was that the *contentious* gap between Israel and the nations had been removed through Christ. His gospel turned ex-pagan Gentiles into holy people who were now brought near to the Jewish God and the Jewish people. Historically, Paul's interpreters have almost entirely agreed that, for the apostle, the gospel includes the elimination of Jewish and Gentile identities. Ironically, the exact opposite is the case.

Central to Paul's gospel is the establishment of prophetic harmony between both Jews and Gentiles. The word "both" implies difference and mutuality. Paul's emphasis is unity, not uniformity. Again, Woods provides a helpful perspective: "The biblical concept of 'one' does not necessarily mean a singularity or homogeneity, but it allows for the unity of distinct elements. . . . Ephesians identifies Gentile believers with Israel, not as Israel. Paul retains distinction between the two in this letter as he does in his other writings."[109]

For Paul, the shalom expressed *between* Christ-following Jews and Gentiles would serve as evidence that the kingdom vision of the Jewish prophets had arrived. If either is not present and distinguishable, or if hostility remains between the two groups, then it's not the end-times kingdom Paul read about in his Bible.

WHERE WALLS GO UP

On the ground level, Christians frequently agree that Jews and Gentiles continue to maintain their identities within the church. And it's not unusual for Christian pastors to express gratitude for having Jewish Christians, also called Messianic Jews, in their congregations. Frequently, I meet Christians who tell me something like, "Hey, we have a Jewish guy in our church. It is so cool how he continues to value his Jewish heritage as a Christian." Such sentiments are not universal, but they are common. And Jews in churches appreciate this.

All this to say, many Christians are okay with and even support the idea that Jews continue to identify as such within the church. So it's all good . . . until a certain threshold is crossed.

It's fine in many Christian communities to identify as a Jew. But when a Jewish Christian says they are obligated to observe the Torah as an expression of Jewish identity, that's where there is frequent, and sometimes painful, pushback. The walls go up.

Long ago, I experienced this personally.

A SPECIAL RULE

My spiritual journey is not the focus of this book. But I sprinkle in personal details, anecdotes, and stories because I have lived at the intersection of Judaism and Christianity as much as I have studied it. And I hope some of my stories have made you smile as we wind through this high-stakes topic that is frequently difficult to navigate.

Well, I also experienced a not-so-cheery story along my path when I was actively participating in Christianity. And it illustrates the dormancy of Paul's rule in modern times.

As I've shared, I was born and raised Jewish. In college, I became an evangelical Christian. But shortly after that, I embarked on a long, bumpy road that led me back to practicing Judaism. Through my religious travels, I have maintained a strong personal connection to Jesus and the New Testament—but I see both in ways significantly different from what is found in normative Christian theology and practice. Of course, I am being very brief here. A fuller account of my story is for another time.

The part of my story pertinent to our discussion on Paul's weird rule is this: A church once denied my membership because I believed that, as a Jewish Christian, I was obligated to keep the Torah—not for my salvation, but as a way of life for me as a Jew seeking to live faithfully to God.

At the bedrock level, in my opinion, I was denied membership because Paul's rule was not—and has not been—understood and practiced by this or any church for most of the past two thousand years. So let's press in and try to sort out what happened.

At the time, I complied and aligned with all aspects required for membership in this church. And the church's membership documents said nothing about Torah observance. However, because the pastor knew me personally and was familiar with my beliefs about Torah observance for Jews, the church denied my membership. Ironically, the church came up with a special rule to deny me membership because I kept the Torah as a Jewish Christian.

As we consider my "special rule" story, there are several vital things to grapple with. First, the pastor would have been okay with welcoming me as a member if I had simply identified as a Jew. It was living as a Jew that he had a problem with. The pastor told me I would only be able to join the church if I renounced my conviction that Torah observance played a significant role in my life as a Jewish follower of Jesus. And I remember his exact words as he summed up our conversation in his office. My view regarding keeping the Torah, he said, was "a threat to the gospel." Again, many Christians are okay with Jews in the church. But when Jews in the church start doing Jewish stuff found in the Torah, that's when it's common for walls to go up.

I imagine some readers may think this pastor's actions were deplorable. Others may think he was justified in denying me membership. And I'm sure some of you are not sure. Each of those reactions, and others that fall in between, are understandable. That leads to my next point.

The second thing we should grapple with from this "special rule" story is that, in my opinion, the pastor in my account should not be demonized. Not even close. Actually, I understand and sympathize with why he and the church made a special rule to deny me church membership. The pastor was protecting a well-established border.

Christian anti-Judaism is deeply embedded within the church and has been from the early days of the Jesus movement. In the early second century, the church father Ignatius said, "It is monstrous to talk Jesus Christ and to live like a Jew."[110] Ignatius's sentiments quickly became the norm in the church. And while such vile, crude language is not the norm in modern times, the viewpoint that undergirds his wording is alive and well.

By denying me membership in the church, though the membership process did not address Torah observance, the pastor's stance protected a line that was first drawn in the church by its earliest post-New-Testament-era leaders. That line is this: Judaism and Christianity are two different religions—and the Torah does not define the marching orders for any followers of Jesus, Jewish or otherwise.

The initial line the early ekklesia drew was quite thin, given substantial evidence that the border between Christians and Jews was anything but thick in the first several hundred years of the Jesus movement. In fact, the line between the Jesus movement and Judaism was quite porous. Various fragments within ancient sources indicate plenty of Christians positively engaged with Judaism and the synagogue in the first few centuries of nascent Christianity. As the historian Karin Zetterholm notes, "That many [Jesus-oriented Gentiles] were involved in Jewish practices, celebrated Jewish festivals and frequented the synagogue is evident from Christian polemical literature and from fourth-century church councils prohibiting such practices."[111]

But in the generations following Paul and his contemporaries, the parting of the ways between Judaism and Christianity grew increasingly wide. And one group in particular regularly found itself in a pressurized zone: Jewish Christians.

It would take hundreds of years into the Common Era for the church to come to a consensus on this group. Eventually, the church adopted a universal viewpoint that Jewish Christians who live Jewishly, as defined by the Torah, are not welcome.

Oddly—and some would say prophetically—in the past hundred years, and especially within the past few decades, this viewpoint is slowly changing. Christians are becoming more aware and accepting of Jewish Christ-followers because, for various reasons, they are once again growing in numbers. Despite modern trends, however, it's still quite unusual for a pastor or church to welcome a Torah-observant Jewish Christ-follower.

But perhaps there are some good reasons for pastors and Christian leaders to consider being weird in this way. And that brings us to the third point to wrestle with as we process my "special rule" case. And I'll frame this one with a question: Would the *historical* Jesus or the *historical* Paul have been welcomed as members of the church that rejected me?

Of course, the Jesus and Paul presented in mainstream, traditional Christian theology would be welcome in that church, and just about every other church. But what about the Jesus and Paul who continued living as faithful Jews?

It's weird to consider this, but I think the answer is clear: Because Paul's rule—which guards both Jewish and Gentile expression within the church—is a foreign concept in Christian practice, I don't think either Jesus or Paul would be granted membership in most churches—in the past or the present.

Paul's weird rule initially served to affirm Gentile identity within the ekklesia because, as we have emphasized, Gentiles following Christ as Gentiles was far from a given. But as the ekklesia quickly became primarily Gentile, this concern became less germane. But remember that Paul's rule affirms Jewish identity within the church as well—and that side of Paul's rule has been anything but a given over most of church history. Paul's rule has largely been ignored and forgotten—which has dramatically affected how Jews have been treated both inside and outside of the church.

Strangely, because Jesus and Paul were Torah-observant Jews, they would likely find a similar reception if they tried to join the church I had. Understandably, most Christians will read this and gasp, "Of course Jesus and Paul could be members of my church!" It's absurd for a Christian to imagine otherwise.

But what if Jesus and Paul insisted on observing the Sabbath, the Jewish holidays, the kosher dietary laws, and the other Torah commandments Jews must keep as a way of life according to God's word? In communities that made an effort to honor Paul's rule, this would be possible. But what about churches that don't even know such a rule exists? This, I'm afraid, would be a problem. Because here's the thing: Jesus and Paul, according to the New Testament, did insist upon and live Jewish lives as defined by the Torah. Thus, to join any community, such a calling would need to be affirmed. As Messianic Jewish scholar Mark Kinzer notes in his groundbreaking book *Postmissionary Messianic Judaism*, "We have good grounds for upholding the view that the New Testament as a whole treats Jewish practice as obligatory for Jews."[112]

DIFFERENCE WITHOUT DISCRIMINATION

So, I shared this story to illustrate a crucial point about Paul's rule. His rule has a practical, tangible expression to it. And it's the practical part, typically, that is hard for Christians to get their minds around.

Remaining in your calling, as a Jew and as a Gentile within the church, means there are some identifiable differences in how each goes about living lives of holiness within the family of God. Differences and distinctions are very different from discrimination. The former can be expressed with respect and unity. The latter leads to painful outcomes, such as being denied church membership because of a different calling.

This sounds like it would be an excellent conference theme! I can imagine it in bright lights at Mercedes-Benz Stadium in Atlanta: *Differences and distinctions without discrimination: A modern discussion on Paul's weird rule.*

Hey, I'd buy a ticket to that—even if it was only with a few people at my Starbucks across the street rather than with thousands at a big arena. Regardless of the size, that, I have no doubt, would be a game-changing conference.

Before we end our discussion on Paul's rule, we need to peek into such a conference that took place roughly two thousand years ago in Jerusalem. This small gathering was a game changer for the early Jesus movement. It affirmed the ideals expressed in Paul's rule and, quite literally, changed the world.

CHAPTER 9

Paul's Weird Rule, Part 2

A gathering that changed the world

THE CONFERENCE (AND CONCERT) OF ALL CONFERENCES (AND CONCERTS)

mentioned how much I love the band U2 at the beginning of chapter 8. As of this writing, I have yet to see them in concert. Another favorite band of mine—who was also influenced by U2— is Coldplay.

But my wife, Kara, and I have something against Coldplay. Seeing Coldplay in concert absolutely ruined us. That sounds negative, but here's the deal. The Coldplay concert was so amazingly good that all other concerts we have seen since that night at Mercedes-Benz Stadium in Atlanta pale in comparison.

Coldplay's lead singer, Chris Martin, was electric. He connected with the audience like no entertainer I have ever seen. And the sound, the lights, the energy . . . it was off the charts. For three hours, it was like we were off the ground. And when they sang "Sky Full of Stars"—okay, I'll stop. You get the point. We loved the Coldplay concert.

Now, don't get me wrong. Kara and I still go to see live music all the time—both big concerts and small, local gigs. But when it comes to big concerts, we can't help but compare them to what we experienced with Coldplay. Truly, that set the standard.

Things are a bit different and complicated regarding the Jerusalem Council. The standard-setting Jerusalem Council was a gathering that should have had an unforgettable impact on the consciousness and memory of the following generations of Christ-followers. And this should not have been so difficult, because a summary of the Jerusalem Council is recorded in Acts 15.

But I imagine some readers are scratching their heads and wondering, "Geez, this Jerusalem Council thing sounds pretty important, but I'm not quite remembering what it was all about. What was the deal there?" If that represents anything close to your thinking, you are normal.

So here's the deal: The Jerusalem Council was a gathering of the first generation of leaders in the Jesus movement. They met in Jerusalem to debate and decide whether non-Jews had to become Jews to have a fully justified standing within the family of God. This conference had tremendous implications not only for Paul's gospel, but for world history.

WHAT HAPPENED IN JERUSALEM . . . WAS NOT SUPPOSED TO STAY IN JERUSALEM

Decisions made at the Jerusalem Council not only stuck but changed the trajectory of Western Civilization. But a pivotal outcome of this gathering has been largely ignored. So, let's dig into this one-of-a-kind historical event. I think you'll see why it was so important—and what needs to be recovered from it as we seek to understand Paul's weird rule.

Until the Jerusalem Council, there was ambiguity regarding the role of non-Jews in the emerging Jesus movement. Remember, the early Jesus movement was an entirely Jewish movement. Most Jews were surprised by the growing number of non-Jews expressing interest in the Jesus movement. And that raised lots of questions for them: Did Gentiles have to become Jewish? How could a pagan sinner be transformed into a holy, righteous person? If Gentiles were joining the family of God, were they equal in standing to Jews?

These questions are weird for us. But they would have been normal and pertinent for first-century Jews who were part of, observing, or affected by the Jesus-following Jewish subgroup that was rapidly attracting and adding non-Jews.

Paul's letters, particularly Galatians, reveal different Jewish answers to those questions. And the other answers and solutions to "the Gentile question" caused significant tension within the early Jesus movement. Acts corroborates the tension detected in Paul's letters. And in Acts 15:1, Luke described a situation that sums up the tension on the ground: "But some men came down from Judea and were teaching the brothers, 'Unless you are circumcised according to the custom of Moses, you cannot be saved.'"

I encourage you to read all of Acts 15. It's a pivotal moment in world history. And here's what was happening: Some Jewish Jesus-followers from Judea (likely from Jerusalem) were teaching the new

Gentile believers in Antioch that they had to be circumcised (become Jews) to be "saved." This was not an isolated incident based on what we read in Paul's letters and what happens next in the Acts 15 narrative.

Acts tells us the leaders of the early Jesus movement gathered in Jerusalem to resolve what they likely appraised to be a problem that threatened the well-being, and perhaps the existence, of the movement. The heavy hitters in the early Jesus movement were there: Peter, Barnabas, James, and, of course, Paul.

With all these strong personalities in the room, it should be no surprise that things got heated. Acts 15:7 records that there was "much debate." But, eventually, they came to a consensus when James stepped forward and announced, "Therefore my judgment is that we should not trouble those of the Gentiles who turn to God" (Acts 15:19).

As Acts presents it, this statement from James ends the debate. I'm sure plenty of folks disagreed with his judgement. Nonetheless, Luke recorded that an official letter was crafted and sent out, which clarified that Gentiles should not be "troubled," meaning they do not have to become Jews to be part of the community of the righteous.

We cannot overstate the massive importance of this decision. The early Jewish leaders of the ekklesia easily could have gone in a different direction and affirmed other Jesus-following Jews who argued Gentiles *did* need to become Jews to be saved.

Imagine if that had been the official ruling. Requiring male non-Jewish followers of Jesus to be circumcised would have severely restricted the spread of the Jesus movement. As Jewish scholar Michael Wyschogrod noted:

> From Acts 15 and elsewhere, we learn that a segment of the Jerusalem church believed that gentiles who wished to belong to the Jesus fellowship had to be circumcised and had to accept all of the [Torah's] commandments. Paul disagreed and believed that Jesus-believing gentiles did not first have to become Jews and only then could they consider themselves followers of

Jesus. Had this view prevailed, Jesus-believing Jews would have remained a small Jewish sect and Christianity would probably not have conquered the Western world.[113]

Conversion to Judaism is a tall order—not to mention a painful one for males—being that circumcision is required to complete the process. Understandably, the number of converts to Judaism has been relatively few for most of history. If early ekklesia leaders had judged that Gentiles must become Jews as part of the gospel, it may well be that the Jesus movement would have fizzled out within a generation or two.

But in Jerusalem, this matter was settled—at least on paper. Gentiles could experience redemption with the Jewish God apart from circumcision and through Jesus alone. This decision positioned the Jesus movement to grow rapidly and exponentially among non-Jews. And that's precisely what happened. As Bart Ehrman noted in his book *The Triumph of Christianity*, "Before four centuries had passed, these twenty or so lower-class, illiterate Jews from rural Galilee had become a church of some thirty million. How does a religion gain thirty million adherents in three hundred years?"[114]

Ehrman's book offers a well-researched answer to a great question. And keep in mind that there's no way Ehrman's question would be asked in the first place if not for the result of the Jerusalem Council.

But there's a component of Acts 15 that is rarely emphasized. This aspect of the judgment largely remained in Jerusalem, though it was intended to be remembered as a central principle for the ekklesia moving forward. The Council's call to action included concrete steps in the form of four prohibitions for non-Jews that would promote unity, but not uniformity, with the Jewish people, whose spiritual family they had been adopted into. With James still serving as the speaker at the meeting, he said the following:

Therefore my judgment is that we should not trouble those of the Gentiles who turn to God, but should write to them to abstain from the things polluted by idols, and from sexual immorality, and from what has been strangled, and from blood. For from ancient generations Moses has had in every city those who proclaim him, for he is read every Sabbath in the synagogues. (Acts 15:19–21)

So, James said Gentile Jesus-followers should not be "troubled," meaning they should not be pressured to become Jews. However, James and the Council presented several Torah-based requirements for non-Jews in verse 20:

1. Don't eat meat sacrificed to idols.
2. Don't engage in sexual immorality.
3. Don't eat meat that has been strangled.
4. Don't consume blood.

Each of these four prohibitions has a basis in the Torah and has multiple Torah commandments associated with it.[115] And, very importantly, these Torah commandments/categories would allow Gentiles to have a smoother enculturation process into Jewish space. Remember, non-Jews were entering a Jewish movement and space at this time—not the other way around.

So, here's what I want you to see for now. James and the Jerusalem leaders expected the Gentile Jesus-followers would observe some of the Torah, not all of it. Keeping all of the Torah would effectively turn Gentiles into Jews. As Daniel Lancaster says in his book *The Holy Epistle to the Galatians*:

Paul himself made a clear line of distinction between Jewish and Gentile believers. In his worldview, Jewish believers are obligated to the covenant responsibilities incumbent upon them. Gentiles are also obligated to God's Torah, but not to those particular aspects of it which define a person as Jewish (such as circumcision).[116]

How much Torah did the early Jewish leaders of the ekklesia expect Christ-following Gentiles to keep? They didn't spell that out in detail.[117] But based on Acts and Paul's letters, Gentiles were taught to keep at least some of it.[118]

But there is an important, fundamental component of the Jerusalem Council that is frequently overlooked. As you can imagine, I would not miss the opportunity to probe the Weird Apostle on this as we continue our discussion at From the Earth.

WHAT WAS IT LIKE TO BE THERE, PAUL?

With impeccable timing, the Petty cover band is now playing the song, "I Won't Back Down." It's like they knew the perfect song to lead into my next question. This is another strange, sublime moment I will remember about the night.

"It's funny, Paul, 'I Won't Back Down' seems to nail it regarding the approach you had at the Jerusalem Council. Truly, you had to stand your ground. Can you tell me what it was like to be there?" I ask.

He smiles and slightly nods. "It sure was a big moment on a lot of levels. And yes, big personalities were in the room. Peter was there. And James. And even some of my fellow Pharisees—a few of whom I grew up with. On a personal level, this was very meaningful. At that point, my role in the movement was controversial—being that I was focused on promoting Jesus to non-Jews. But at that gathering in Jerusalem I strongly sensed my role was being publicly affirmed. I had met with some of the characters in that room previously, but there I felt affirmed in my emphasis that non-Jews in Christ are fully accepted members of God's family—even though not everyone in the room agreed. Things were tense at that meeting. I had to battle for the position I stood for. But I knew what was right. And honestly, Ryan, that moment gave me the confidence boost I needed. I had no doubt about my calling and emphasis. But it's tough and lonely to be passionate about something that is opposed by people you respect."

My mind races. Many assume Paul is an unstoppable, relentless force oozing with confidence. Some would even argue he is arrogant and intractable. Whether or not those descriptions are accurate, I am seeing a different side of him—a very human side—with insecurities just like the rest of us. I feel like I am riding a wave. I have to keep him talking.

"Paul, as you alluded to, your view about the standing of non-Jewish Christ-followers was affirmed in Jerusalem. And that was huge. But what about the Jewish side of things?" I ask. "Are there some implications regarding Jews that have been obscured, misrepresented, or forgotten from that gathering?"

He doesn't flinch or hesitate in responding. "Yes, and it grieves me. We were only there to discuss whether Gentiles coming to embrace our God and our way of thinking needed to go all the way and become Jews. There is no question that we needed to clarify how Gentiles would relate to things like circumcision and keeping the Torah. But it never crossed our minds that anyone in the Jesus movement would doubt if Jews needed to practice circumcision and keep the Torah. That was a given. If Jews don't practice circumcision and keep the Torah, what's left to tangibly define them as Jews? We never doubted for a minute that Jews would continue to live as Jews—be they followers of Jesus or not. That, Ryan, has been forgotten and severely distorted. As it sounds like you are well aware of . . . lots of folks after my time concluded that because we discouraged circumcision and full Torah observance for Gentiles, we were doing so for everyone. That simply was not the case."

This might be the most important thing Paul has said all night.

BACK TO MY WORDS

The Jerusalem Council was predicated on the assumption that Jews, Jesus-followers or not, *do* keep the Torah as a way of life. It's because of this that there was debate about whether in-Christ Gentiles needed to do the same. If Jews didn't have to keep Torah anymore because of Christ, everyone would have understood that Gentiles didn't have to either.

At this point, things may be a bit confusing. And this is too big to miss. So, let's sum up where we are: James and the others gathered in Jerusalem assumed Jews kept the Torah in full. In Acts 15, the Jerusalem Council made a decision and wrote a letter highlighting parts of the Torah that Gentiles needed to be mindful of. Paul, in his letters, presented more Torah instruction specific to Gentiles.

And here's the important point from both Acts and Paul. Although Jews and Gentiles are meant to be unified in Christ, their unique callings come with different responsibilities concerning Torah observance. They are one but not the same.

So we see here that the Jerusalem Council decision harmonizes with Paul's rule in 1 Corinthians 7, which emphasized that Jews remain as Jews and Gentiles remain as Gentiles, and each should keep the commandments that applied to them. The Jerusalem Council decision made it clear that in-Christ Gentiles should not become Jews. Future generations received that part of the message loud and clear.

What those generations didn't receive was the Council's assumption that Gentiles would keep parts of the Torah, but not in exactly the same ways Jews do. Isaac Oliver explains this with precision:

> According to Acts, the "Jerusalem Council" established that Gentile followers of Jesus did not need to keep the entire Torah but only four commandments. However, this verdict was reached under the assumption that Jewish followers of Jesus would continue to uphold the Torah in all facets. Nowhere in Acts are Jews granted license to abandon their ancestral practices.[119]

The Jerusalem Council decision, which protected Gentile identity within the ekklesia, carried forth from Jerusalem and positioned the church to triumph the Western World. But its instructions for Gentiles to observe sections of the Torah, which allowed for unity with their Jewish brothers—for whom it was assumed were keeping the Torah in full—were forgotten.

It's hard to say what came first—the Jerusalem Council decision or Paul's rule in all the churches. But they affirmed the same concept from a different angle. Within the family of God, Jews remain as Jews and Gentiles remain as Gentiles. Each has different commandments they are responsible for keeping. They are one but not the same. This, for Paul, would evidence that the kingdom of God, that same kingdom he read about in his Bible, had broken into this world.

HOW DOES THIS CHANGE THE GAME?

From where we stand, it seems odd to think Paul and the early leaders of the ekklesia had to be so adamant about non-Jews *not* becoming Jews within the Christ movement. I mean, geez, there had to be an entire conference about this!

And Paul had to communicate a decisive rule to promote unity and distinction between Jewish and Gentile followers of Jesus. But it wouldn't take long for his rule to be largely ignored, if not forgotten.

This is all a bit bizarre. But it also makes sense.

After Paul's lifetime, the ekklesia became increasingly Gentile as the number of Jews at both the leadership and ground level of the movement rapidly decreased. While there is evidence of Jewish, Torah-observant groups within the church into the fourth and fifth centuries, our sources point to the church being overwhelmingly Gentile by the early second century. And with a Gentile-dominated church, for most practical purposes, Paul's rule became antiquated. There simply were not many Jews around to advocate for the Jewish branch of the Jesus movement. Holger Zellentin, a scholar of late antiquity, says, "It appears that very few Church Fathers seem to have endorsed the distinction between Jewish and Gentile ethnicity and therefore between Jewish and Gentile law that marked the Acts of the Apostles and other New Testament texts."[120] The second, third, and following generations of leaders within the Jesus movement rarely emphasized Paul's rule.

Slowly but surely, the Jesus movement evolved from a subgroup within Judaism to an entity that was theologically and relationally divorced from the Torah, Judaism, and Jews. And thus the church, as an entity distinct from Jews and Judaism, was born.

But an almost unfathomable thing has happened in recent generations. Paul's weird rule is being reintroduced and reconsidered by Jewish and Christian scholars and historians. And it is a big reason that the game is changing and Paul is being reframed as both the apostle to the Gentiles *and* as an advocate for the Torah and Judaism for Jews.

For most of the past two thousand years, Paul has been presented as the apostle who collapsed all differences between Jews and Gentiles. Christianity replaced Judaism. Grace replaced the law/Torah. And Christian identity not only superseded but eliminated Jewish identity for sure—and some would say Gentile identity as well. That's the familiar version of Paul.

But Paul is being allowed to speak again. And for many, it represents a massive shift in how both Christians and Jews understand Paul—and how the relationship between the two groups can improve.

Paul's weird rule ensured followers of Jesus would be one but not the same. And the unified, diverse ekklesia, according to Paul, would represent the dawning of a new, prophetic era. As Pamela Eisenbaum has aptly noted:

> Just as the lion lies down with the lamb, so the Jew and the Gentile come together in peace and harmony. To envision the world to come as a time of peace among all the peoples of the world is to envision a world where there still exists many different peoples, for there would be no significance to the image of peace if in the world to come there is only one nation.[121]

Making Paul's rule *not* weird gives us a very different version of Paul. It also gives us a different view of the church and the possibilities regarding relations between Christians and Jews.

GAME-CHANGING ACTION

This book is not designed to prescribe a detailed course of action for the church or the synagogue. But it's also not meant to simply fill minds with information.

If we make Paul weird again, both Christians and Jews will inevitably grapple with that and consider how a fresh take on the apostle affects things on the ground. In most cases, such grappling will start with Christians—because Paul's letters are part of their Bibles. How Christians understand Paul affects how they apply his letters. And how Christians apply Paul's letters historically affects how Christians interact with Jews and Judaism. When Jews start seeing changes in how Christians interact with them, they will want to know the source of the catalyst. This has been the pattern with the reclamation of the Jewishness of Jesus. And it can be the case with Paul as well.

Reconsidering Paul's rule and its modern implications has great potential to enrich the lives of both Christians and Jews—especially the relationship between them. Currently, it is a standard assumption in the Jewish community that Paul was an enemy of Judaism. Abolishing the Torah was central to his gospel. Most Jews who know anything about Paul assume this to be indisputable. Understandably, many Jews would think that if Paul had a rule, it probably included something contrary or negative toward Judaism.

But what if that narrative turned upside down? What if the Jewish community began seeing that Paul encouraged Jews *to live* as Jews regardless of their convictions about Jesus? What would happen if the standard Jewish assumption about Paul was that he loved the Torah, kept the Torah, and assumed other Jews—be they followers of Jesus or not—would do the same? What if the ideas of Pamela Eisenbaum, a Jewish scholar who is not a follower of Jesus, became mainstream within the Jewish community? Ideas like this one:

> Readers have largely presumed that Paul's embrace of Christ necessarily involves a rejection of Torah, and so they have read his letters through this lens. . . . There is no denying that Paul had some sort of profound religious experience through which he became a believer in Jesus. . . . But this experience did not cause him to turn away from Judaism. . . . Nothing less than an entirely new framework is needed to interpret what Paul says about the law.[122]

Far from rejecting the Torah, Paul's rule upheld the Torah for Jews but did not require Gentiles to keep it in the same way Jews do. As someone who lives and worships in the Jewish community, I can confidently say the new framework Eisenbaum envisions would go a long way in helping Jews have greater respect for Christianity and their Christian neighbors.

A reappraisal of Paul's rule could also have tremendous implications for the Christian community. First, Paul's rule demonstrates that the ekklesia was never designed to be monolithic. Paul's rule promotes unity and diversity between Jews and Gentiles within the ekklesia. It also implies that diversity within those categories is healthy.

Paul affirmed that his ekklesiae in the Gentile world looked different from location to location. Along this line, I find the modern emphasis on multicultural churches interesting. I've spent plenty of time at individual churches that were very diverse. And if different cultures are comfortable finding a unified expression that works for their community, that's beautiful. However, it's also healthy for there to be predominantly black churches, Korean churches, Latino churches, and white churches. Paul's universal gospel offers the opportunity for diverse cultures to create unique local expressions within their churches. And not only does Paul seem to be okay with that, but he seems to think varied expressions reflect the strength of the broader ekklesia rather than hinder it. In Paul's mind, that God, through Jesus, unifies diverse people indicates bigness, not smallness.

But there's another side to Paul's rule for the modern church that is important to explore: the role of Jews in churches. Historically, many Jews have ended up in churches for various reasons. Jews visit or join churches because of a Christian spouse. Some have Christian friends who invite them to church and it sticks. And some end up in churches because they become committed followers of Jesus. Regardless of the reason, lots of Jews are in churches.

But churches typically lack the encouragement for Jews to live as Jews within the church. What if things were different? What if the "special rule" story I told in the last chapter, in which I was denied membership in a church because of my commitment to living as a Jew, went in the opposite direction? What if the pastor had said this instead: "We affirm your Jewish faith and want to support you as a Jewish believer in our predominantly Gentile church. Though we can't provide a fully Torah-observant environment, we'll be respectful, sensitive, and positive toward your faith. Paul's teaching encourages Jews to live as Jews and Gentiles as Gentiles. Let us help you be the best Jew you can be."

That right there would be a game changer. Gentile Christians encouraging Jews to live as Jews within the church would be a massive step toward recovering Paul's rule in all the churches. This dynamic would also create a bridge between Christians and Jews, the church and the synagogue. Jews living as Jews within churches would provide a tangible link for Christians to connect with the Jewish people and the Torah—a link Paul never envisioned would be broken.

Paul's weird rule was designed to promote unity, not uniformity. With U2, he would happily sing along to "One."

CHAPTER 10

The Weird Apostle for Today

1-percent improvements

'm a big fan of James Clear, the author of the bestselling book *Atomic Habits*.¹²³ His weekly *3-2-1 Newsletter*¹²⁴ is one of the few emails I read every time.

One of Clear's big ideas is that small changes can lead to remarkable results. I love his emphasis on 1-percent daily improvements. When you are consistent with small improvements, the little things add up to something incredible over time. Here's a classic Clear statement:

It is so easy to overestimate the importance of one defining moment and underestimate the value of making small improvements daily. Too often, we convince ourselves that massive success requires massive action. Whether it is losing weight, building a business, writing a book, winning a championship, or achieving any other goal, we put pressure on ourselves to make some earth-shattering improvement that everyone will talk about. . . . Meanwhile, improving by 1 percent isn't particularly notable—sometimes it isn't even noticeable—but it can be far more meaningful, especially in the long run.[125]

Clear's "1-percent improvement" idea is good to keep in mind as we wrap up and consider how to apply *The Weird Apostle* in our daily lives. The last thing you should do is throw out all you know and have learned about Paul. I doubt I have been so persuasive that you would do so. But even if you found every page in this book convincing, earth-shattering changes in your thinking and approach to Paul may not move the needle much.

The familiar view of Paul is deeply established in Jewish and Christian culture. It will take time to shift the narrative. Thus, it's important to focus on the long game when it comes to making Paul weird again. But this is worth it—even if we only focus on 1-percent improvements. Here's why.

1. Restoring Paul to his first-century Jewish and Greco-Roman context can help Christians.

For Christians, Paul is indispensable. Paul's letters are preached, taught, and studied more than any other section of the Bible. And largely, Christians form their view of Jesus and the gospel through the filter of Paul's letters. If you are significantly off in how you understand Paul and his letters, it can negatively affect how you understand Jesus and the gospel. Thus, a more historical and biblical view of Paul is of great importance for Christians, even if that makes him (and Christians) a little weird.

2. Restoring Paul to his first-century Jewish and Greco-Roman context can help Jews.

Jews mostly ignore Paul. When they do give him attention, it's typically with unfavorable reviews. These negative views of Paul, however, are based mainly on Christian misrepresentations of Paul that we have discussed in this book. As we noted, though, an increasing number of Jewish thinkers are not waiting for Christians to restore Paul to his Jewish context. Much progress is being made by Jewish (and non-Jewish) scholars to restore Paul "within Judaism." These pioneers are currently minority voices. But that is changing.

There are many benefits to the Jewish community broadly reappraising Paul, as many have already done with Jesus. Most Jews disagree with Paul regarding Jesus's identity. However, Jews have many things to learn from their brother Paul—especially from his efforts to help non-Jews experience the wisdom of the Torah and its vision for global peace and repair.

3. Restoring Paul to his first-century Jewish and Greco-Roman context can help improve relationships between Christians and Jews.

Paul had no idea Judaism and Christianity would develop into two distinct religions. Most scholars would agree with that statement. More open to debate is whether the seeds for "the parting of the ways" are present in the New Testament.

My take is that with the passage of decades and generations, it was inevitable and healthy that the Jesus movement assumed its own structure and forged its own identity as an entity distinct from Judaism. Paul and other New Testament writers were clear that faithfulness to God included prioritizing devotion to Jesus. Thus, it was inescapable that the Jesus movement would take steps to create its own space for a blooming of identities—especially non-Jewish ones—who pledged allegiance to that banner. It simply was not feasible for non-Jewish Jesus-followers to walk out their devotion to God within the space of the Judaism of the rabbis in the generations following the New Testament era.

However, what *was* avoidable was the hostility that mounted between Jews and Christians as time marched on. The Judaism and Christianity we now know developed concurrently in the generations following the destruction of the Jerusalem Temple in 70 CE. However, both developed viewpoints and internal boundaries that all too often served as a negative and protective response to the other. Thus, the two paths, from a relational standpoint, diverged.

But perhaps the space between the two parallel movements could have been characterized by a sense of kinship and respect. History sure would have gone differently if that had been the case. Of course, we can't rewrite the story. But we can chart a new course and develop a new narrative in which our destinies converge, rather than remain separated. Paul is key to this.

The traditional view of Paul guarantees that the space between Christians and Jews remains cold and densely populated with thickets and marshland. But if we restore Paul to this context and make him weird again, the land between the two paths can be not only hospitable but gratifying to traverse. If such convergence were to occur, daylight would remain between Christians and Jews. But that daylight would shine through warm air for both groups to breathe as they stand side by side. In an increasingly polarized and isolated world, such unity seems to be of mutual benefit and interest to both entities.

BACK AT FTE . . . IT'S TIME TO PAY THE BILL

Though it's been a while since the sun set over the trees on Holcomb Bridge Road, I only now notice it's getting chilly at our table. I usually put on a jacket as soon as the sun disappears, but I've been too engrossed in the conversation to sense the drop in temperature.

We've been at the table for a while. There's so much more I want to discuss. But Paul needs to go. I'm grateful he gave me as much time as he did. The conversation started a bit bumpy, but the Weird Apostle settled down and became enjoyable to talk to.

"Paul, before we go, I have two questions—" I start to say, but then the server appears with the bill. Paul doesn't move, so I grab it. I'm sure he has the money—or does he? But he seems deep in thought and in another realm. I am happy to take care of it. It feels strange to pay for Paul's dinner, but strange is par for the course with this guy.

"Okay, back to my questions. The first one is, can we do this again? The second one is, what message would you want people to hear today—something timely and urgent you would like to share if you could?"

Paul looks up. He takes a breath and looks back down to my level. "More than anything, at this time, I want people to know my life was dedicated to bringing peace, not division. I paid a high price to spread the idea that the God of Israel is full of love, mercy, and compassion for all people. Jesus also paid a high price for that idea—which I discuss a lot in my letters. It grieves me that my letters have been used too often as a weapon. And I'm blown away that there has been so much discord between the followers of Jesus and my Jewish family. This has to change. And I think if people better understood what I was saying, that could happen. I'm going to leave it there. Because the rest is not up to me; it's up to Christians and Jews to repair the breach that I never envisioned or intended.

"Oh . . . and yes, we can do this again sometime."

I wrote this book with the hope that it will help Christians and Jews to do "the rest"—1 percent at a time.

And one more thing.

Where will I meet the Weird Apostle for that next conversation? You'll have to wait for the next book for that answer . . .

POSTSCRIPT

There's much more to discuss about *The Weird Apostle*. In the follow-up volume to this book, I plan to explore the following:

- Paul's weird expectations (for non-Jews)—Paul, the Jewish teacher of Torah for Gentiles.
- Paul's weird letters—Paul was a letter-writer, not a theologian.
- Paul's weird statements—Paul's most difficult statements (and there are plenty!).
- Paul's weird communities—Paul planted Jewish subgroups for non-Jews, not churches as we know them.

And more . . .

Here are some "1-percent" steps you can take to stay connected and informed about what's next:

1. Sign up for my *Game Changers Email* at www.ryanlambertforum.com for short and sweet game-changer ideas and videos about Paul and other topics.
2. Follow me on social media:
   Facebook: @ryan.lambert.52493
   Instagram: @ryan_lambert_atl
   YouTube: @RyanLambertForum
3. Contact me with questions or invitations to speak at www.ryanlambertforum.com.

ACKNOWLEDGMENTS

The inspiration, help, and encouragement I received before and during the writing process for *The Weird Apostle* came from many directions. Space won't allow me to include everyone who contributed. But I have a good memory. And I won't forget those who helped in some way, whether you are mentioned here or not.

Joseph, Anna, Esther, Jesse, and Naomi: The book is finally done! Can you believe it? No more talking about it. Each of you, in your own way, is a game changer. And you are why I tell people I am a five-time millionaire. I love every second with you. Always.

Doc, thanks for reading this and giving your detailed feedback. Starbucks on Holcomb Bridge will never be the same. A lot of those chats led to this book.

Tony, you were there when I needed perspective and encouragement. And I appreciate the important edit you made to this manuscript. You are a good soul.

Debora, you cheered me on from day one when I started writing. And you wisely advised me not to overthink things—especially when I was dizzy at the end of the process. Thank you. And, yes, you can hand-deliver a signed copy to him.

Derek, you read this manuscript with super attentive eyes. I appreciate your investment. It made this book stronger. You, my friend, are going to do great things.

D, my bro, it meant a lot that you read through this with all you are juggling. You understand the issues and the stakes. Your feedback was invaluable. And I treasure our friendship.

Mark, you will be remembered for many things, not the least of which is generosity with your time. Considering the season, your willingness to dedicate bandwidth to this project means a lot.

David, thank you for reading this book and sharing your honest thoughts. Your work is incredibly important. And our conversations and friendship enrich my life.

Ruth, somehow you reviewed this as a busy mom with a full-time job. I appreciate that. What you said about how this book impacted your view of Paul touched me.

Dave, you are an example of the solution to many of the problems I discussed in this book. Christians like you, who are repairing what was broken, are changing the game. I'm thankful for you, mate.

Karen, thank you for being so helpful in getting this book to the finish line. You are a delight to work with and put me at ease. I will enthusiastically refer other self-publishing authors to you!

Alyssa, I am thankful for you—my on-the-ball, thoughtful editor. You dug into this project and made it so much better. Thank you.

And, Mom, though it wasn't your style, you would have liked a good bit of this book—especially the stories and songs. You would also be happy with how I've evolved in my understanding of Judaism, God, Jesus, and Paul. What I wouldn't do to be able to hand you the first copy. You've been gone way too long. But I'll see you again.

Kara: This book is already dedicated to you, but that isn't enough. This book doesn't happen without you. You are a gift from heaven to me and so many others.

And you're the one that I call home.

ENDNOTES

1   In the world of Pauline scholarship, seven of the thirteen letters attributed to Paul in the New Testament are considered undisputed. The seven letters that scholars agree Paul wrote are Romans, Galatians, Philippians, 1 Corinthians, 2 Corinthians, 1 Thessalonians, and Philemon. This does not mean Paul didn't write the other six letters attributed to him in the New Testament. It simply means it is disputed among scholars whether Paul, or an individual or group claiming to be Paul, wrote these letters. Of the six disputed letters, quite a few scholars include Ephesians and Colossians as authentically written by Paul. Most scholars consider 2 Thessalonians, 1 Timothy, 2 Timothy, and Titus as not written by the apostle. In *The Weird Apostle*, I interact mostly with Paul's undisputed letters and Ephesians. However, I also engage the disputed letters at times and work under the assumption that, authentic or not, the disputed letters reflect thinking consistent with Paul's outlook and can be harmonized with the undisputed letters.

2   Daniel R. Langton, *The Apostle Paul in the Jewish Imagination* (New York, NY: Cambridge University Press), 17.

3   2 Peter 3:16.

4   Matthew V. Novenson, *Paul Then and Now* (Grand Rapids, MI: Eerdmans), 5.

5   Two important works that highlight the work of scholars within this camp are Mark D. Nanos and Magnus Zetterholm, *Paul within Judaism* (Minneapolis, MN: Fortress Press, 2015); Karin Hedner Zetterholm and Anders Runesson, *Within Judaism?* (Lanham, MD: Fortress Academic, 2024).

6   Matthew Thiessen, *A Jewish Paul* (Grand Rapids, MI: Baker).

7   I plan to continue this conversation in a follow-up book. This is subject to change, but I am currently preparing to cover the following in volume 2: Paul's weird expectations (for non-Jews), Paul's weird letters, Paul's weird statements (difficult passages in his letters), Paul's weird communities, and more! To stay updated regarding volume 2 and other projects, please sign up for my email newsletter at www.ryanlambertforum.com.

8   Yes, yes, I know that at times Crosby, Stills & Nash also included a Neil Young in the mix. The song in view in this chapter, "Wasted on the Way," did not include Young and is attributed to Crosby, Stills & Nash only.

9   Galatians 1:13–14.

10   2 Corinthians 11:23–28.

11   With Peter/Cephas in Galatians 2:11 and with Barnabas in Acts 15:36–41.

12   Sholem Asch, *The Apostle* (New York: G.P. Putnam's Sons), 79–80.

13   Christians are sometimes surprised that many scholars question the historical reliability of Acts. The authorship of Acts is also debated. Acts is not my specialty, but I do see it as a reliable source. Clearly, Acts has a theological and ideological agenda. It is not merely a historical account. But it's not unusual for scholars who question the reliability of Acts to still quote it as a

useful source. My objective or interest is not to defend or debate the details of Acts. For this book, I operate under the assumption that Acts is reliable and that Luke is the author. For great stuff on Acts from a Jewish perspective, I highly recommend the work of Isaac Oliver and Mark Kinzer. For a Christian perspective on Acts, Craig Keener's work is indispensable.

14 Pamela Eisenbaum's comments on questioning whether Josephus was a Pharisee are helpful: "In spite of the fact that he gives an account of the three Jewish schools (Pharisees, Sadducees, and Essenes) in his first major work, the War, which recounts the history of the revolt . . . he never says he is a Pharisee. Thus, scholars rightly wonder whether he really was a Pharisee, or whether it simply became expedient for him to claim the title at a much later point in life." Pamela Eisenbaum, *Paul Was Not a Christian* (New York, NY: Harper Collins), 131.

15 Adam Grant, *Think Again* (New York, NY: Viking).

16 Pamela Eisenbaum, *Paul Was Not a Christian* (New York, NY: Harper Collins), 125.

17 Josh Moody, "Your Inner Pharisee." www.thegospelcoalition.org/article/your-inner-pharisee. The article posted on The Gospel Coalition website on August 11, 2017.

18 Peter Haas, *Pharisectomy* (Springfield, MO: Influence Resources, 2012).

19 Andy Stanley, *Not in It To Win It* (Grand Rapids, MI: Zondervan), 155–156.

20 See Kent Yinger's *The Pharisees* (Eugene, OR: Wipf and Stock, 2022); Joseph Sievers and Amy-Jill Levine, *The Pharisees* (Grand Rapids, MI: Eerdmans, 2021); Richard A. Horsley, *The Pharisees and the Temple-State of Judea* (Eugene, OR: Wipf and Stock, 2022).

21 The Hebrew phrase used for this group in the Dead Sea Scrolls is דּוֹרְשֵׁי חֲלָקוֹת, *doreshei ḥalakot*. It appears in several Dead Sea texts, particularly in fragments 3 and 4 of Pesher Nahum from Qumran Cave 4.

22 Pamela Eisenbum, *Paul Was Not a Christian* (New York, NY: Harper Collins), 120–121.

23 Ibid., 131.

24 Kent L. Yinger, *The Pharisees* (Eugene, OR: Cascade), 152.

25 Richard A. Horsley, *The Pharisees and the Temple-State of Judea* (Eugene, OR: Wipf and Stock), 43.

26 Kent L. Yinger, *The Pharisees* (Eugene, OR: Cascade), 176.

27 Even before Stendahl, scholars such as Johannes Munck and W. D. Davies took Paul's Jewish and Pharisaic identities seriously.

28 Both essays can be found in Krister Stendahl, *Paul Among Jews and Gentiles* (Minneapolis, MN: Fortress).

29 Ibid., 15.

30 For a thorough treatment of the range of viewpoints regarding conversion among Jews in Paul's time, see Matthew Thiessen, *Contesting Conversion* (New York, NY: Oxford University Press).

31   See Paula Fredriksen's essay "Paul, the Perfectly Righteous Pharisee" in Sievers and Levine's *The Pharisees* (Grand Rapids, MI: Eerdmans), 132–133.

32   Translation by Paula Fredriksen, ibid., 126.

33   See Mark Nanos's essay "Paul and Judaism" in *Reading Paul within Judaism: The Collected Essays of Mark D. Nanos, Volume 1* (Eugene, OR: Wipf and Stock), 29–30.

34   See Paula Fredriksen's essay "Paul, the Perfectly Righteous Pharisee" in Sievers and Levine's *The Pharisees* (Grand Rapids, MI: Eerdmans), 133.

35   See Isaac Oliver's essay "The Calling of Paul in the Acts of the Apostles" in Oliver and Boccaccini's *The Early Reception of Paul The Second Temple Jew* (New York, NY: T&T Clark), 187–188.

36   David Christian Clausen, *Meet Paul Again for the First Time* (Eugene, OR: Wipf and Stock), 95.

37   Michael Wyschogrod, *Abraham's Promise* (Grand Rapids, MI: Eerdmans), 236.

38   Paula Fredriksen, *Paul: The Pagans' Apostle* (New Haven, CT: Yale University Press), 34.

39   Various ultra-orthodox, Chassidic Jewish groups claim to have ongoing interactions with deceased *tzaddikim* (thoroughly and unusually holy or righteous individuals). In particular, visiting the *ohel* (burial site) of a tzadik is thought to be a reliable way to open a channel of communication with the tzadik.

40   By "Jewish Bible," I am referring to what Christians label as the Old Testament. Jewish Bibles include the same thirty-nine books in the Old Testament section of Christian Bibles. However, in Jewish Bibles, the ordering of the individual books differs.

41   John G. Gager, *The Jewish Lives of the Apostle Paul* (New York, NY: Columbia University Press), 12–13.

42   For more on Mark Nanos, check out his website at www.marknanos.com.

43   Michael Wyschogrod, *Abraham's Promise* (Grand Rapids, MI: Eerdmans), 200.

44   The term "New Perspective on Paul" was first popularized through a highly influential essay and lecture delivered by Dr. James Dunn in 1982 in the Manson Memorial Lecture at the University of Manchester. Dunn has since released a book titled *The New Perspective on Paul* (Grand Rapids, MI: Eerdmans, 2007).

45   E. P. Sanders, *Paul and Palestinian Judaism* (Minneapolis, MN: Fortress), 181.

46   Pamela Eisenbaum, *Paul Was Not a Christian* (New York, NY: Harper Collins), 63.

47   Excerpted from *The Complete Artscroll Siddur* (Brooklyn, NY: Mesorah Publications), 125.

48   See www.ryanlambertforum.com for more on my engagement with these topics.

49   Actually, I've done a little more than dabbling. As of this writing, I also manage the marketing and public relations for my son's awesome Atlanta-based company, *Joseph's Junk Removal* (www.josephsjunkremoval. com).

50   Paula Fredriksen, *Paul: The Pagans' Apostle* (New Haven, CT: Yale University Press), 148.

51   Quoted from the essay "Paul and Israel" by Matthew Thiessen and Paula Fredriksen in *The Oxford Handbook of Pauline Studies* (Oxford, United Kingdom: Oxford University Press), 8.

52   Lionel Windsor, *Reading Ephesians and Colossians after Supersessionism* (Eugene, OR: Wipf and Stock), 165.

53   Quoted from the essay "Paul and Israel" by Matthew Thiessen and Paula Fredriksen in *The Oxford Handbook of Pauline Studies* (Oxford, United Kingdom: Oxford University Press), 4.

54   *ESV Study Bible* (Wheaton, IL: Crossway), 2309.

55   Abraham Joshua Heschel, *The Prophets* (New York, NY: Harper & Row), 367.

56   In Jewish terminology, the present age is referred to as *Olam Ha-Zeh* (literally, "this world or age") and *Olam Ha-Ba* ("the world to come").

57   David Christian Clausen, *Meet Paul Again for the First Time* (Eugene, OR: Wipf and Stock), 140.

58   Jamie Davies, *The Apocalyptic Paul* (Eugene, OR: Wipf and Stock), xxvi.

59   Paula Fredriksen, *Paul: The Pagans' Apostle* (New Haven, CT: Yale University Press), 132.

60   Ibid., 73.

61   Matthew Novenson, *Paul, Then and Now* (Grand Rapids, MI: Eerdmans), 52–53.

62   *Shabbat* is a Hebrew word for "sabbath."

63   For more on the Society of Biblical Literature (SBL), check out www. sbl-site.org.

64   Pamela Eisenbaum, *Paul Was Not a Christian* (New York, NY: Harper Collins), 212.

65   Matthew Thiessen, *A Jewish Paul* (Grand Rapids, MI: Baker).

66   If readers know of renderings, even unpopular ones, that portray a Jewish-looking Paul, I welcome you to reach out and let me know at www.ryanlambertforum.com.

67   Thomas R. Schreiner, *Paul, Apostle of God's Glory in Christ* (Downers Grove, IL: Intervarsity Press), 55–56.

68   Jewish kosher dietary (kashrut) practices are based on biblical commandments found in Leviticus 11 and Deuteronomy 14.

69   Some assume ancient and modern Jews who keep kosher will only dine in homes that also keep kosher. This is not necessarily the case. Ancient sources reveal examples of Jews and non-Jews dining together—presumably with accommodations for the Jewish guests if the meal took place in a non-Jewish home. And in modern times, some observant Jews are more than happy to dine in an environment that does not normally maintain

kosher standards—if modifications are made, which usually involves bringing kosher food from the outside into the environment where Jews are the guests.

70   Sinek's talk can be viewed at www.ted.com/talks/simon_sinek_how_ great_leaders_inspire_action.

71   Simon Sinek, *Start with Why* (New York, NY: Penguin Group), 39.

72   Thomas R. Schreiner, *Paul, Apostle of God's Glory in Christ* (Downers Grove, IL: Intervarsity Press), 57.

73   John G. Gager, *The Jewish Lives of the Apostle Paul* (New York, NY: Columbia University Press), 96.

74   See Isaac Oliver's essay "The Calling of Paul in the Acts of the Apostles" in Oliver and Boccaccini's *The Early Reception of Paul The Second Temple Jew* (New York, NY: T&T Clark), 187.

75   Quoted by David Rudolph in his essay "Luke's Portrait of Paul in Acts 21:17–26" in Oliver and Boccaccini's *The Early Reception of Paul The Second Temple Jew* (New York, NY: T&T Clark), 197.

76   Ibid., 198.

77   Two books that emphasize the centrality of Jerusalem in Luke-Acts and in Paul's general thinking include Mark S. Kinzer, *Jerusalem Crucified, Jerusalem Risen* (Eugene, OR: Wipf and Stock, 2018), and Isaac W. Oliver, *Luke's Jewish Eschatology* (New York, NY: Oxford University Press, 2021).

78   John Barclay, *Paul & the Gift* (Grand Rapids, MI: Eerdmans), 359–360.

79   *ESV Study Bible* (Wheaton, IL: Crossway), 2297.

80   Lionel Windsor, *Reading Ephesians and Colossians after Supersessionism* (Eugene, OR: Wipf and Stock), 216.

81   *ESV Study Bible* (Wheaton, IL: Crossway), 2252.

82   In personal correspondence with Mark Nanos, he reminded me that he makes the point about the noninclusion of "weeks" and "Sabbaths" in Paul's list in Galatians 4:10, which points to Paul having pagan practices in mind in the text. Nanos makes this argument in his book *The Irony of Galatians* (Minneapolis, MN: Fortress Press, 2002), yet he also informed me that he owed the basic insight (though developed differently) to Troy Martin's article "Pagan and Judeo-Christian Time-Keeping Schemes in Gal 4:10 and Col 2:16" in the journal *New Testament Studies*, Issue 42 (New York, NY: Cambridge University Press, 1996), 120–132.

83   Joe Slunaker, bibleproject.com/articles/temple-of-god.

84   Pamela Eisenbaum, *Paul Was Not a Christian* (New York, NY: Harper Collins), 156.

85   "Jacob" is not the real name of my softball friend.

86   John MacArthur, *The MacArthur Study Bible* (Nashville, TN: Thomas Nelson Publishers), 1710.

87   An excellent, thorough, non-supersessionist treatment of 1 Corinthians 9:20–23 is David Rudolph's *A Jew to the Jews*.

88   For more on Mark Nanos, please visit www.marknanos.com.

89   Amy-Jill Levine and Marc Zvi Brettler, *The Jewish Annotated New Testament, Second Edition* (New York, NY: Oxford University Press).

90   Mark D. Nanos and Magnus Zetterholm, *Paul Within Judaism* (Minneapolis, MN: Fortress Press).

91   There is a growing list of scholars who identify as Christians and are part of the Paul within Judaism movement. Early voices include Anders Runesson, Karin H. Zetterholm, William S. Campbell, Kathy Ehrensperger, Neil Elliott, and Gabriele Boccaccini. More recent names include Rafael Rodriguez, Genevive Dibley, Frantisek Abel, John Van Maaren, Christopher Zoccali, Brian Tucker, and Matthew Thiessen. David Rudolph, who identifies as a Messianic Jew, also writes within this paradigm.

92   Mark D. Nanos, *Reading Corinthians and Philippians within Judaism* (Eugene, OR: Cascade Books), 103.

93   Ibid., 99.

94   See www.chabad.org.

95   A number of Jewish organizations now exist to help Christians learn the Torah from a Jewish perspective. Examples include www.root-source.org, led by Gidon Ariel, and www.israel365.com, led by Rabbi Tuly Weisz. Orthodox Jewish influencer David Nekrutman has also published an unprecedented work to guide Christians in how to celebrate the Sabbath (*Your Sabbath Invitation*, USA: David Nekrutman, 2022). www.alephbeta.org is another Jewish teaching entity, led by Rabbi David Fohrman, that many Christians are turning to—though Aleph Beta still primarily orients its teaching toward a Jewish audience. Christian or messianic groups that specialize in helping Christians learn the Torah include First Fruits of Zion (www.ffoz.org); Fusion Global, led by messianic Rabbi Jason Sobel (www.fusionglobal.org); Ahavat Ammi Ministries, led by messianic Rabbi Yitzchak Shapira (www.ahavatammi.org).

96   Matthew Novenson, *Paul, Then and Now* (Grand Rapids, MI: Eerdmans), 186.

97   James Dunn, *The Epistle to the Galatians* (Grand Rapids, MI), 205.

98   *ESV Study Bible* (Wheaton, IL: Crossway), 2251.

99   D. Thomas Lancaster, *The Holy Epistle to the Galatians* (Marshfield, MO: First Fruits of Zion), 194.

100   Brian Tucker, *Remain in Your Calling* (Eugene, OR: Wipf and Stock), 78.

101   N. T. Wright, *Paul and the Faithfulness of God* (Minneapolis, MN: Fortress Press), 1435.

102   It is important to note the work of Rosen-Zvi and Ophir on the topic of how Paul used the term "Gentile" (Greek, *ethne*) in what seems to be a new and uniquely general manner. These scholars posit that before Paul, Jews and others used this term in reference to specific *ethne*—such as Greeks, Romans, Egyptians, etc. But Paul tended to use the term in a non-differentiated way with reference to the general category of nations to mean "non-Jews." This is the way later rabbinic writers used the term as well. And it's interesting to consider, which Rosen-Zvi and Ophir suggest, that Paul may have been the trailblazer in using the term "Gentile" to designate the broad category of Gentile(s). Nonetheless, Paul still evidences values that allow for diversity and uniqueness within the generalized category of

Gentile(s). See the essay "Paul and the Invention of the Gentiles" by Ishay Rosen-Zvi and Adi Opher in *The Jewish Quarterly Review*, Vol. 105, No. 1 (Winter 2015), 1–41.

103   Paula Fredriksen, *Paul: The Pagans' Apostle* (New Haven, CT: Yale University Press), 164.

104   R. Kendall Soulen, *The God of Israel and Christian Theology* (Minneapolis, MN: Fortress Press), 169.

105   See the essay "Paul and the Invention of the Gentiles" by Ishay Rosen-Zvi and Adi Opher in *The Jewish Quarterly Review*, Vol. 105, No. 1 (Winter 2015), 21.

106   John Barclay, *Paul & the Gift* (Grand Rapids, MI: Eerdmans), 567.

107   William S. Campbell, *The Nations in the Divine Economy* (Lanham, MD: Lexington Books/Fortress Academic), 134.

108   David B. Woods, "Jew-Gentile Distinction in the One New Man of Ephesians 2:15," *Conspectus* 18 (2014), 123.

109   Ibid., 126–127.

110   Ignatius of Antioch, *Letter to the Magnesians 10:3*. www.orderofstignatius. org/files/Letters/Ignatius_to_Magnesians.pdf.

111   See the essay "Jesus within Third- and Fourth-Century Judaism" by Karin Hedner Zetterholm in *Within Judaism?* (Lanham, MD: Fortress Press), 219.

112   Mark S. Kinzer, *Postmissionary Messianic Judaism* (Grand Rapids, MI: Brazos Press), 95.

113   Michael Wyschogrod, *Abraham's Promise* (Grand Rapids, MI: Eerdmans), 232.

114   Bart Ehrman, *The Triumph of Christianity* (New York, NY: Simon & Schuster), 7.

115   Isaac Oliver has persuaded me that these four prohibitions are based on Leviticus 17–18, which details purity laws for non-Jews living among Jews. Oliver says, "Lev 17–18 contain laws relevant for both Israelites and resident aliens, and readily presents itself as a model that could be appropriated and adapted for incorporating Gentile followers of Jesus into the early ekklesia. All four items in Luke's version of the decree can be paired with laws appearing in Lev 17–18." Isaac Wilk Oliver, *Torah Praxis after 70 CE* (Eugene, OR: Wipf and Stock), 394.

116   Daniel Lancaster, *The Holy Epistle to the Galatians* (Marshfield, MO: First Fruits of Zion), 193.

117   See Daniel Nessim's *Torah for Gentiles* (Eugene, OR: Wipf and Stock) for a well-researched presentation on how the Jewish authors of "The Didache" provided guidance to the early Gentile disciples of Jesus on how to keep the Torah *as Gentiles*.

118   2 Timothy 3:16 states, "All Scripture is breathed out by God and profitable for teaching, for reproof, for correction, and for training in righteousness, that the man of God may be complete, equipped for every good work." When this was written, only the Hebrew Scriptures/Old Testament were categorized as Scripture. Thus, this text offers evidence that early Christian training used the Torah and the entire Old Testament to "train"

Christ-followers with the goal of making them "complete, equipped for every good work."

119   Isaac Wilk Oliver, *Torah Praxis after 70 CE* (Eugene, OR: Wipf and Stock), viii.

120   Holger M. Zellentin, *Law Beyond Israel* (Oxford, United Kingdom: Oxford University Press), 19.

121   Pamela Eisenbaum, *Paul Was Not a Christian* (New York, NY: Harper Collins), 98.

122   Ibid., 212–213.

123   James Clear, *Atomic Habits* (New York, NY: Penguin Random House).

124   You can sign up for the *3-2-1 Newsletter* at www.jamesclear.com.

125   James Clear, *Atomic Habits* (New York, NY: Penguin Random House), 15.

BIBLIOGRAPHY

Asch, Sholem. *The Apostle*. New York: G.P. Putnam's Sons, 1943.

Barclay, John. *Paul & the Gift*. Grand Rapids, MI: Eerdmans, 2015.

Campbell, William S. *The Nations in the Divine Economy*. Lanham, MD: Lexington Books/Fortress Academic, 2018.

Clausen, David Christian. *Meet Paul Again for the First Time*. Eugene, OR: Wipf and Stock, 2021.

Clear, James. *Atomic Habits*. New York, NY: Penguin Random House, 2018.

Davies, Jamie. *The Apocalyptic Paul*. Eugene, OR: Wipf and Stock, 2022.

Dunn, James. *The Epistle to the Galatians*. Grand Rapids, MI, 1993.

Ehrman, Bart. *The Triumph of Christianity*. New York, NY: Simon & Schuster, 2018.

Eisenbaum, Pamela. *Paul Was Not a Christian*. New York, NY: Harper Collins, 2009.

ESV Study Bible. Wheaton, IL: Crossway, 2008.

Fredriksen, Paula. "Paul, the Perfectly Righteous Pharisee." In *The Pharisees* by Joseph Sievers and Amy-Jill Levine. Grand Rapids, MI: Eerdmans, 2021.

Fredriksen, Paula. *Paul: The Pagans' Apostle*. New Haven, CT: Yale University Press, 2017.

Gager, John G. *The Jewish Lives of the Apostle Paul*. New York, NY: Columbia University Press, 2015.

Grant, Adam. *Think Again*. New York, NY: Viking, 2021.

Haas, Peter. *Pharisectomy*. Springfield, MO: Influence Resources, 2012.

Harvey, Richard S. *Luther and the Jews*. Eugene, OR: Wipf and Stock, 2017.

Hedner Zetterholm, Karin and Anders Runesson. *Within Judaism?* Lanham, MD: Fortress Academic, 2024.

Heschel, Abraham Joshua. *The Prophets*. New York, NY: Harper & Row, 1962.

Horsley, Richard A. *The Pharisees and the Temple-State of Judea*. Eugene, OR: Wipf and Stock, 2022.

Ignatius of Antioch, *Letter to the Magnesians 10:3*. www.orderofstignatius.org/files/Letters/Ignatius_to_Magnesians.pdf

Kinzer, Mark S. *Postmissionary Messianic Judaism*. Grand Rapids, MI: Brazos Press, 2005.

Lancaster, Daniel. *The Holy Epistle to the Galatians*. Marshfield, MO: First Fruits of Zion, 2011.

Langton, Daniel R. *The Apostle Paul in the Jewish Imagination.* New York, NY: Cambridge University Press, 2010.

Levine, Amy-Jill and Marc Zvi Brettler. *The Jewish Annotated New Testament, Second Edition.* New York, NY: Oxford University Press, 2017.

MacArthur, John. *The MacArthur Study Bible.* Nashville, TN: Thomas Nelson Publishers, 2006.

Moody, Josh. "Your Inner Pharisee." www.thegospelcoalition.org/article/your-inner-pharisee. Article posted on The Gospel Coalition website on August 11, 2017.

Nanos, Mark. *Reading Corinthians and Philippians within Judaism.* Eugene, OR: Cascade Books, 2017.

Nanos, Mark. *Reading Paul within Judaism: The Collected Essays of Mark D. Nanos, Volume 1.* Eugene, OR: Wipf and Stock, 2017.

Nanos, Mark and Magnus Zetterholm. *Paul Within Judaism.* Minneapolis, MN: Fortress Press, 2015.

Nektrutman, David. *Your Sabbath Invitation.* USA: David Nekrutman, 2022.

Novenson, Matthew V. *Paul Then and Now.* Grand Rapids, MI: Eerdmans, 2022.

Oliver, Isaac. "The Calling of Paul in the Acts of the Apostles." In *The Early Reception of Paul The Second Temple Jew* by Isaac Oliver and Gabriele Boccaccini. New York, NY: T&T Clark, 2019.

Oliver, Isaac. *Torah Praxis after 70 CE*. Second printing. Eugene, OR: Wipf and Stock, 2023.

The Complete Artscroll Siddur. Brooklyn, NY: Mesorah Publications, 125, 1984.

Rosen-Zvi, Ishay and Adi Opher. "Paul and the Invention of the Gentiles." In *The Jewish Quarterly Review*, Vol. 105, No. 1 (Winter 2015).

Rudolph, David. "Luke's Portrait of Paul in Acts 21:17–26." In *The Early Reception of Paul The Second Temple Jew* by Isaac Oliver and Gabriele Boccaccini. New York, NY: T&T Clark, 2019.

Sanders, E. P. *Paul and Palestinian Judaism*. Minneapolis, MN: Fortress Press, 1977.

Schreiner, Thomas R. *Paul, Apostle of God's Glory in Christ*. Downers Grove, IL: Intervarsity Press, 2001.

Sievers, Joseph and Amy-Jill Levine. *The Pharisees*. Grand Rapids, MI: Eerdmans, 2021.

Sinek, Simon. *Start with Why*. New York, NY: Penguin Group, 2009.

Soulen, R. Kendall. *The God of Israel and Christian Theology*. Minneapolis, MN: Fortress Press, 1996.

Stanley, Andy. *Not In It*. Grand Rapids, MI: Zondervan, 2022.

Stendahl, Krister. *Paul Among Jews and Gentiles*. Minneapolis, MN: Fortress Press, 1976.

Thiessen, Matthew. *A Jewish Paul.* Grand Rapids, MI: Baker, 2023.

Thiessen, Matthew. *Contesting Conversion.* New York, NY: Oxford University Press, 2011.

Thiessen, Matthew. "Paul and Israel." In *The Oxford Handbook of Pauline Studies* by Matthew Thiessen and Paula Fredriksen. Oxford, United Kingdom: Oxford University Press, 2022.

Tucker, Brian. *Remain in Your Calling.* Eugene, OR: Wipf and Stock, 2011.

Windsor, Lionel. *Reading Ephesians and Colossians after Supersessionism.* Eugene, OR: Wipf and Stock, 2017.

Woods, David B. *Jew-Gentile Distinction in the One New Man of Ephesians 2:15. Conspectus* 18 (2014), 123.

Wright, N. T. *Paul and the Faithfulness of God.* Minneapolis, MN: Fortress Press, 2013.

Wyschogrod, Michael. *Abraham's Promise.* Grand Rapids, MI: Eerdmans, 2004.

Yinger, Kent. *The Pharisees.* Eugene, OR: Wipf and Stock, 2022.

Zellentin, Holger M. *Law Beyond Israel.* Oxford, United Kingdom: Oxford University Press, 2022.

Ryan Lambert is a thinker, writer, teacher, and creator.

He loves exploring game-changing ideas in leadership, relation-ships, health, personal growth, and spirituality—especially in the areas of Jewish-Christian relations, education, and bridge-building.

Roswell, Georgia, just north of Atlanta, is home to Ryan and his wife, Kara. They love time with their family, Braves baseball, the North Georgia mountains, and life close to the Chattahoochee.

Ryan welcomes invitations to speak and teach. You can contact him and sign up for his email newsletter at ryanlambertforum.com.